Rock 'n' Reno II
The Sequel

A scrapbook look at some of the bands and entertainers that kept Reno rockin' 'n' rollin' in the 2nd half of the 20th Century!

Mike Mantor, Gerry Foster McCarroll, and a cast of hundreds!

Rock 'n' Reno II: The Sequel

A scrapbook look at some of the bands and entertainers that kept Reno rockin' 'n' rollin' in the 2nd half of the 20th Century!

Mike Mantor, Gerry Foster McCarroll, and a cast of hundreds!

Also by Mike Mantor and Gerry Foster McCarroll:

"Rock 'n' Reno—A History of the Rock Bands in Reno, Nevada, from the Early 60's to the Early 80's"

Printed by: Kindle Direct Publishing

An Amazon Company

ISBN: 9798394497247

Welcome to Rock 'n' Reno II: The Sequel!

In our first book, we covered a lot of the home-grown, garage bands that had their roots in the Reno music scene of the 60s and 70s. This one has been expanded to also cover the 80s and the 90s.

However, this book does not contain any material featured in the first book. By way of explanation...you may encounter some of the same bands, but none of the same articles or photos will reappear. In some cases, agencies and managers may have re-used the same publicity photos on multiple posters or other advertising. Consequently, you may encounter SOME repeats of photos on more than one entry. But every precaution has been taken to avoid any outright duplication. If, by chance, human error has allowed a duplicate photo or two, we apologize, and please don't hold it against us!

Another change this time around is that we have chosen to include some of the bands who played in the casino lounges, which we did not feature in the last book. In those instances, we have attempted to confine that element to those bands that had roots in Reno, or who relocated here, or appeared here often enough to become an integral part of Reno's nightlife scene.

"The Sequel", like the first book, is not meant to be a complete "encyclopedia", as such, but rather a representation of some of the bands we have partied with.

We've indeed been fortunate to have enjoyed so many talented people over the forty-year span that this book covers, right here in our Biggest Little City.

So, kick back and join us for a look back at some of that great musical entertainment!

Here is a photo of us at our most successful book signing for our first book, at Bizarre Guitar on Nov. 17, 2018: (Photo by David Strelz)

Doesn't our hair look great?

Table of Contents

Jerry Weems
1950-1999

Jack Bedient and the Chessman were one of the most popular bands in Reno in the 60's. They got a lot of radio airplay with hit records, such as "Pretty One" and "Double Whammy".

JACK BEDIENT and the CHESSMEN

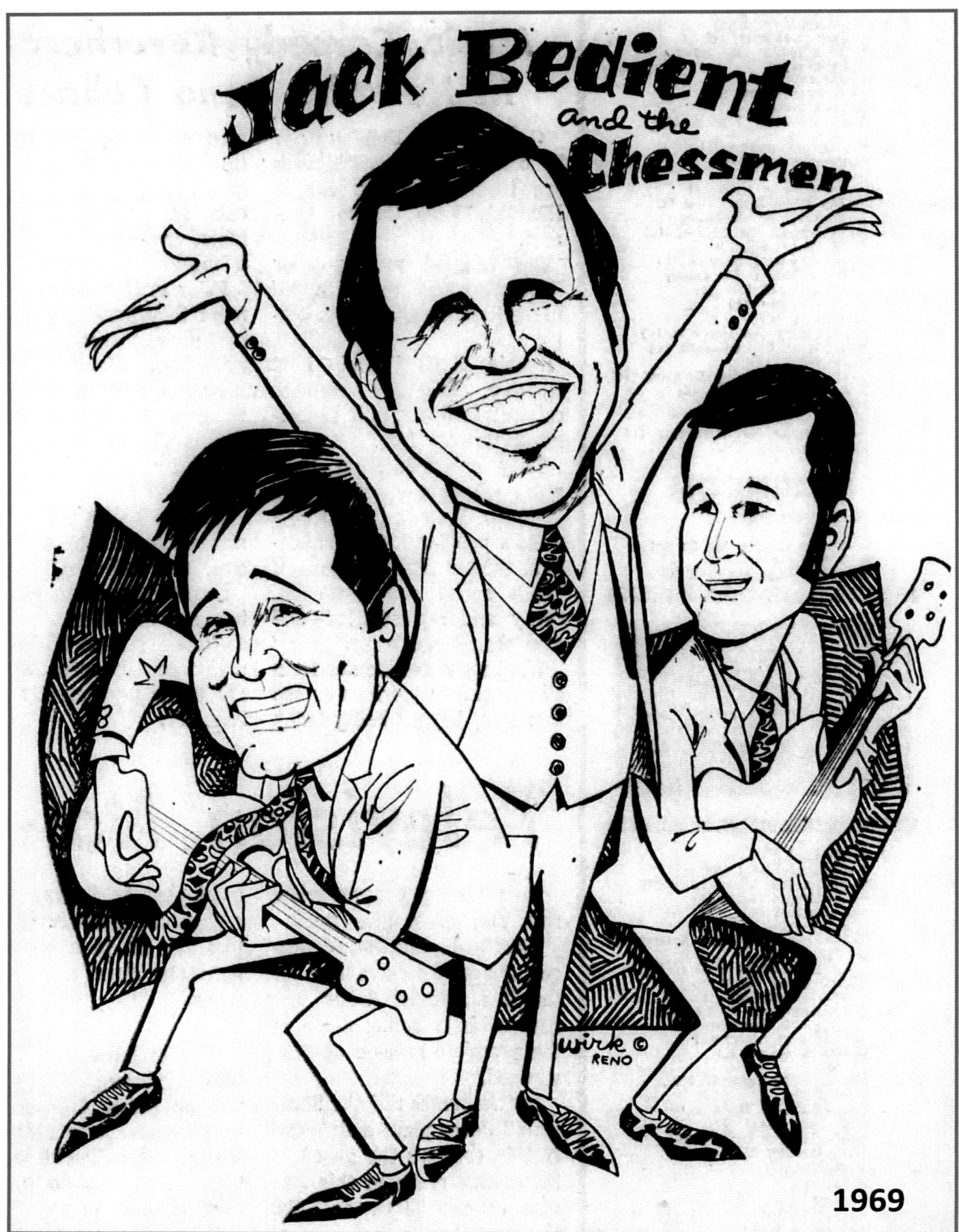

1969

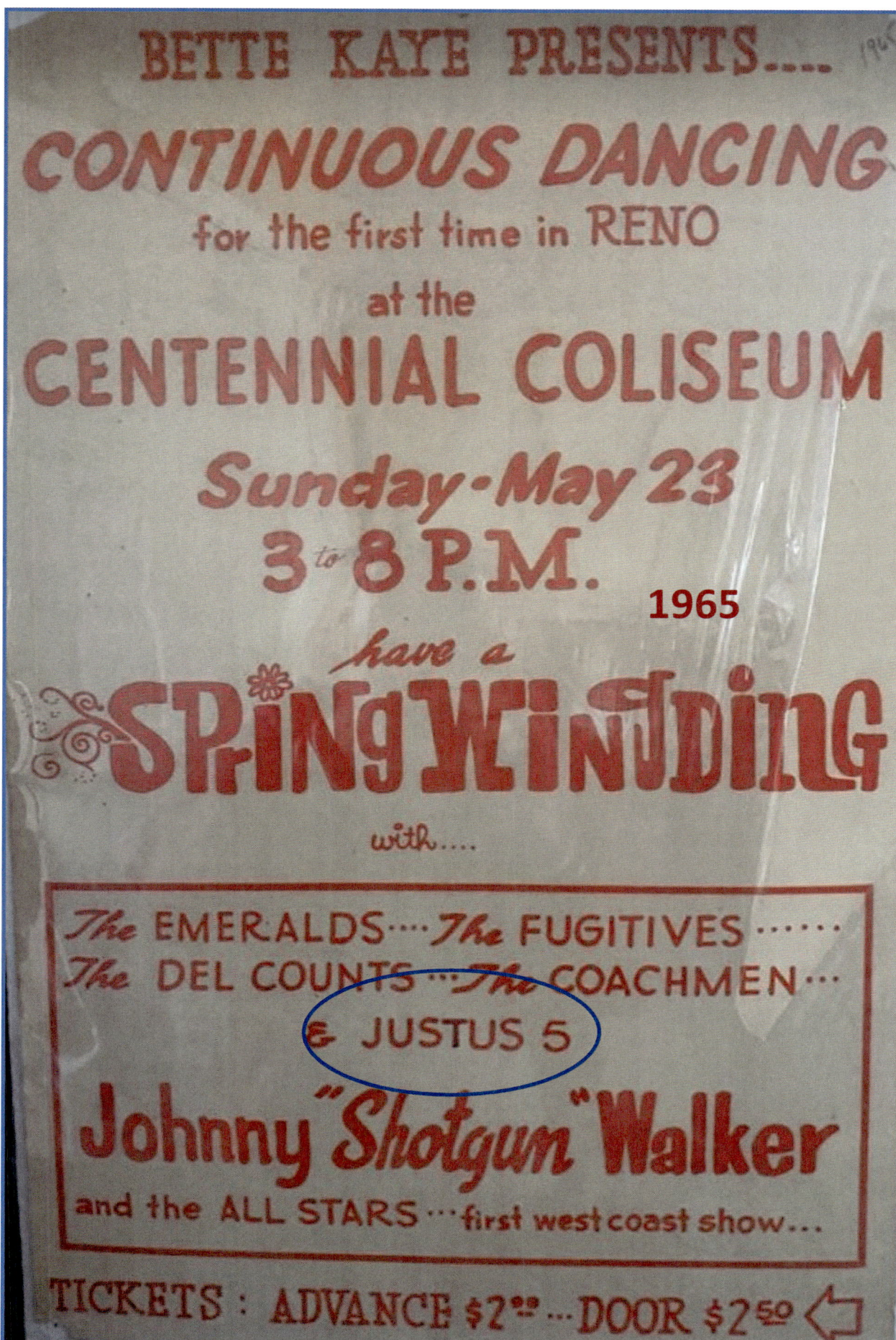

STAGE DOOR JOHNNY
By Mike Mantor

One night in early 1985, I was watching an old movie called "Summer Stock", in which the guys who were hot for the girls in the chorus lines would show up at the stage door with candy and flowers in hopes of procuring a romantic liaison. The girls referred to these horny pursuers as "Stage Door Johnnys." I thought, "what a great name for a band if I ever have another one."

As fate would have it, I got a call to do a crab feed charity event at the Kerak Shrine in Reno a couple weeks away. Having no real band at the time, I made a few calls and cobbled together a 4-piece group to play the gig. It went extremely well, and that same night they re-booked us for the following year's event.

Soon thereafter, I started getting calls for the band to play other events as well as some of the local clubs. Problem was, the other three guys were in other bands and not always available. So, I started the practice of booking the date, then throwing together whoever I could find to play the gigs. I never seemed to have a problem scrounging up unemployed musicians who were happy to make a $100 bill (sometimes more, more often less!). This practice is much more common these days, as it was back in the days when bandleaders culled their band members from the local musician's unions. But...those cats could all read the music handed out to them at the gig. Most of my compadres could not.

I eventually compiled a list of rock standards that most rockers could play without rehearsal, with the key that I did them in noted. Everybody had played "Mustang Sally", "Old Time Rock 'n' Roll", "Born To Be Wild", "Louie, Louie", "Hang On Sloopy", and maybe 40 others so many times they could play them in their sleep (some often did!).

Before long I had collected a book of venues and agents that kept us busy, in addition to the engagements I still booked myself. I had a good "in" at the University of Nevada, and often provided the music for many of their events, from sorority and fraternity parties to "Hello on the Hill", as well as opening shows for national acts. We played most of the local rock clubs (well, at least once!) such as The Grand Ballroom, Little Waldorf, Hacienda del Sol, Bishop's...I recall one particular dive called the "Beer Barrel" up by the university. Lord, what a joint! At one time, the toilet in the men's crapper had been ripped up so many times, there was just an open pipe in the floor...and not every guy who made use of it had perfect aim! A swamp that I took every opportunity to avoid...but sometimes, hey...when ya gotta go...

The most fun I had in this band was opening for name acts, as we did for The Romantics ("What I Like About You" and "Talking In Your Sleep"), The Motels ("Suddenly Last Summer" and "Only The Lonely"), the Pat Travers Band, and a cool "toga party" that featured Otis Day & The Knights from the movie "Animal House." We also became the house band at Paul Revere's Kicks in downtown Reno for a couple of years. Paul himself and his band members dropped in on occasion, and we always had a hoot jamming and partying. We knew each other from the early 80's, when I was with Rob Hanna's Salute to Rod Stewart, and shared many a stage. Bill Medley also came in on occasion.

I'm hesitant to list the musicians who played at least ONE gig with me, from fear I'll forget somebody. But I'm gonna give it a go. If I left out your name, hey...it IS rock 'n' roll, and on any given night who knows what may have been imbibed?

Steve Hobson, Dave Clark, Danny Quintana, John Cleek, Gilbert Trujillo, Fred Myer, Scott Myer, Glen Anthony, Michael Furlong, Glenn Hicks, Latisha Lewis, Danny Leone, Scott Roller, Terry Petersen, Jerry Weems, Steve Hatley, Mark Ishikawa, Ron Barron, Paul Manktelow, Mick Valentino, Derek Smith, Darius Javaher, Skip Gillette, Chuck Ruff, Boris Tavcar, Steve Dunwoodie...and "The Tuna Boats" (Kathy McCovey and Tami Oxford), who occasionally sang backup and sexed up the stage a bit!

Some very fun times, for the most part. My undying gratitude to all those who participated. Good times with good friends.

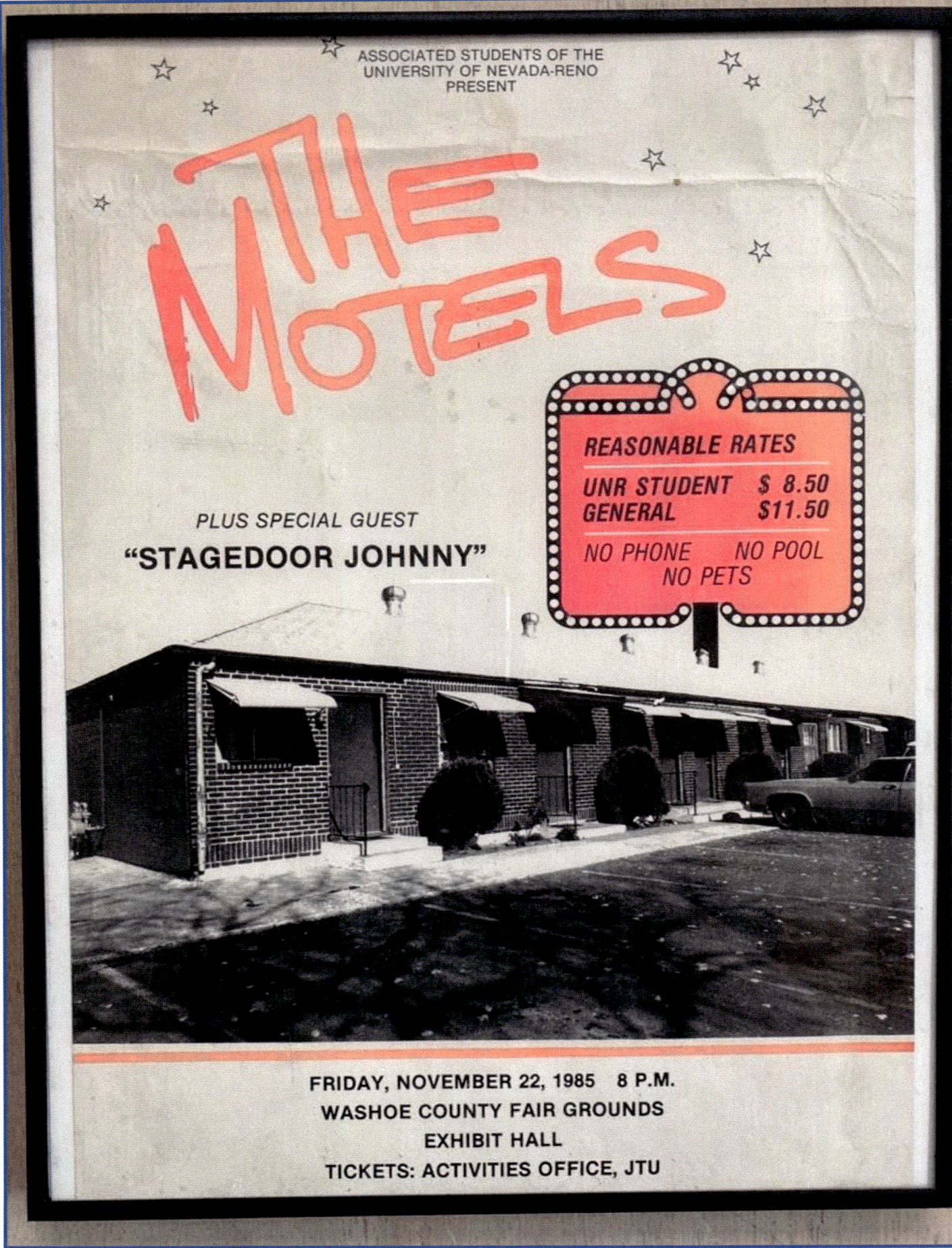

"America's Love Affair With Cars and Rock 'N' Roll"

SUNDAY AUGUST 6, 1989

NOSTALGIA FAIRE
ENTERTAINMENT SCHEDULE

```
12:00 - 12:45------B.B. AND THE BOOME
 1:00 -  1:45

         1:45------SET PAPA CLUTCH

 2:00------------------GRAPE VINE(PAPA CL

 2:00 -  3:15------PAPA CLUTCH

 3:45 -  4:45------STAGE DOOR JOHNNY
 5:00 -  6:00
```

August 3 - 6

"America's Love Affair With Cars and Rock 'N' Roll"

VIP

TOM GERSICH ★ BILL ANTOS ☆ RICKY RUIZ ★

RONNA MILLER ★ JUDY HICKS ★ CARLA VESTBIE

RUDY HERNANDEZ ★ ☆

Invite You To Our
25TH ANNUAL

BIRTHDAY PARTY

NOVEMBER 16TH
6:30 P.M.

HORS D'OEUVRES

NO HOST COCKTAILS

DRIFTWOOD LOUNGE
(Greenbrae Lanes - Sparks)

DANCE TO THE MUSIC OF:
STAGE DOOR JOHNNY
$5.00 PER PERSON

1992

Davis, Motels 'shock' Reno

By Joe DeChick/Gazette-Journal

After spending the better part of this year opening for the likes of Rick Springfield and Supertramp, the Motels checked into the Exhibit Hall of Reno's Nevada State Fairgrounds Friday night as headliners.

Led by sultry songstress Martha Davis, the six-member band from Los Angeles ripped through an 18-song, 85-minute set that more than pleased a meager crowd of approximately 650 people.

After opening with a pair of songs from its fifth and latest album "Shock," the band established the scenario for the rest of the evening with Davis racing the stage, shaking hands and ceaselessly bobbing her black, frizzy mane.

Clad in black from the peak of her fedora to the point of her mukluks, Davis took charge and proved that her charisma, ability to sell a song and sex appeal — refreshingly downplayed — rank with Christine Kerr (the former Chrissie Hynde), Ann Wilson and Pat Benatar.

In fact, she could have sold the Brooklyn Bridge and a truckload of new Coke with her piercing, Liz Taylor eyes alone.

And the voice. Madonna has listened more than once to Davis' bubbly croonings and swanky octave pops.

The superior salesmanship is a must for the Motels, a band that flip-flops from rail-splitting rocker to heart-tugging ballad with nary a chord change.

Review

Although Davis occasionally picked up a guitar, the ax-wielding and synthesizer pumping belonged to the tight five men behind her.

Guy Perry's slashing lead guitar licks highlighted new songs like "State of the Heart" and "Cries and Whispers," as well as the old favorite "Take The L."

Equally rousing were the Jr. Walker-like saxophone wailings of veteran Marty Jourard. Jourard did double duty on the Yamaha, and engaged in a few exciting synth standoffs with keyboardist Scott Thurston — who also brandished a Yamaha — on "Take The L" and the new "Icy Red."

Perhaps the standout tune of the evening was "Shock," the title track from the latest album. Propelled by yet another burbling synth duel and the woodpecker percussion of Brian Glascock, the song orbited Valley Road on the strength of Michael Goodroe's chubby bass, and then landed safely, proving this is the group's most modern song yet.

After closing with the former Top 10 hit "Only The Lonely," the Motels sped through a two-song encore and exited, leaving the distinct impression that they are worthy of headlining, and blowing Springfield off the stage — wherever he is.

Reno's Stagedoor Johnny opened the show with a competent, but anonymous and somewhat sluggish set of hard-rock warhorse covers like "Brown Sugar," "La Grange" and — heaven forbid — "Louie Louie."

21

Miller & ASUN Insanely Present

Otis Day's Birthday Party
& Blowout Toga Bash

Featuring . . .

Prizes
for the
wettest,
skimpiest
& shortest
TOGAS!!!

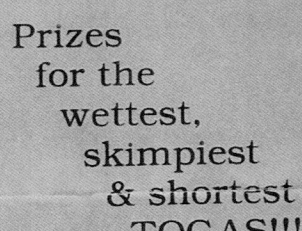

APPROVED
For Posting On
Bulletin Boards
ONLY
Activities Office JTU

The
Party
of 1985!

OTIS DAY
and the Original Animal House Band
and special guest Stagedoor Johnny
Saturday, September 21, 1985
8:30 p.m.
Fairgrounds Exhibit Hall

Tickets available starting Tuesday at the Activities Office, JTU

Students

$3.00

Plus party favors
balloons
refreshments
food

General Admission
(Must be 18 or older)

$5.00

Stage Door Johnny and their pal, "Mickey"

LITTLE WALDORF SALOON
AND GRILL
A TRADITION SINCE 1922
1661 NO. VIRGINIA   323-3682

This Weekend, Live,
Original and Classic rock
With

Stage Door Johnny

Friday & Saturday   10 p.m. 'til ?

"SAGEBRUSH"
3-10-89

Vol. 16, No. 18, April 27-May 3, 1989

Johnny's 'fun-time' tunes

1990

Long before the days of MTV, face-melting heavy metal, disco and boring electronically produced computer music, there was a magic land where Buddy Holly, Elvis Presley, Little Richard, Eddie Cochran, Gene Vincent, Fats Domino, Jerry Lee Lewis and Chuck Berry lived. They made fabulous dance-oriented rock 'n' roll music that was fun to party to.

The next generation spawned its own children — the Beatles, Rolling Stones, Creedence Clearwater Revival, the Beach Boys and the Young Rascals — carrying on in that dance tradition.

Stage Door Johnny brings this era back to life at the Gold Dust West Lodge-Casino through April 30. He re-creates the excitement and energy of all the great songs from that fun time in American music.

Mike Mantor is Stage Door Johnny. Mantor has been performing live rock 'n' roll in the Reno area since 1963, when his band, the Jesters, dropped its surf music format, changed the name to Justice Five and released a record called "Things Get Worse." The record did well regionally and established Justice Five as the top band in the area for several years.

Until it broke up in September 1967, Mantor's band performed hundreds of local proms, sorority-fraternity parties and all the local nightclubs. In addition, the group became the act of choice for concerts, opening dozens of shows for such acts as Beau Brummel, Righteous Brothers, Dick Clark's "Caravan of Stars," Sonny and Cher, the King, Del Shannon, Beach Boys and Johnny Mathis.

Mantor went on to form other groups that performed in the Reno area for the next 20 years. Among them were Long Broad & Swift, Yankee Rose, Banned Aid and the Casualaires. Mantor also performed for four years as a member of Rob Hanna's Salute to Rod Stewart.

In 1986 he put together Stage Door Johnny to play at a friend's wedding. The band was so well received, he decided to keep it together.

For show times, call 323-2211.

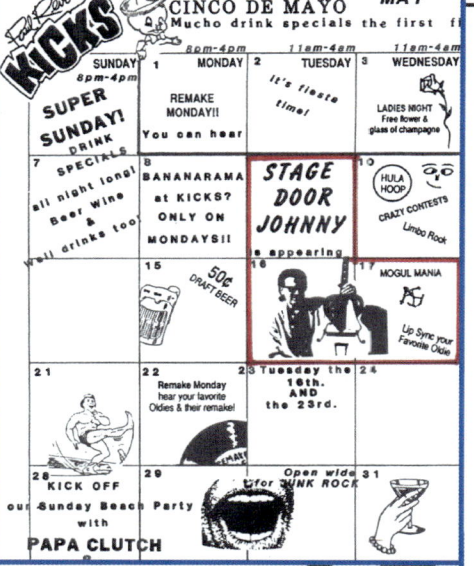

MIKE IS THE ROCK ON WHICH LOCAL ROCK WAS BUILT

<u>Hacienda</u>. Possibly the last of the real Reno musicians, a tall cat with long curly blonde hair plays this local South Virginia Street nightclub.

"Sittin' on the Dock of the Bay," might well be Mike Mantor's own song considering he's played every bar, gig, hangout, hideout, concert, love-in, leave-out; name it, Mike's played it. Like a nemesis that keeps coming back to haunt, Mantor is a Biggest Little City fixture, like the Arch itself. From the Sixties and the State Building to the Burly Bull to nearly every other club that's come and gone in a town full of them, Mantor is like the rock on which local rock and roll was built. Probably the undiscovered Comstock Lode itself.

Mike takes it all with a grain of salt and it's curious that he plays to a packed house here when his last gig midtown barely drew a line in the snow. The crowd has obviously missed the point and is, as always, just out for a good time. But if they keep coming back, what they'll see is the Nemesis himself, Mike Mantor, perennially unpretentious, real.

There are times when real identity is better left alone, undiscovered, so that it won't spoil. Such is the case of <u>Mike Mantor</u>, onstage with <u>Stagedoor</u> Johnny at the Hacienda del Sol on South Virginia St.

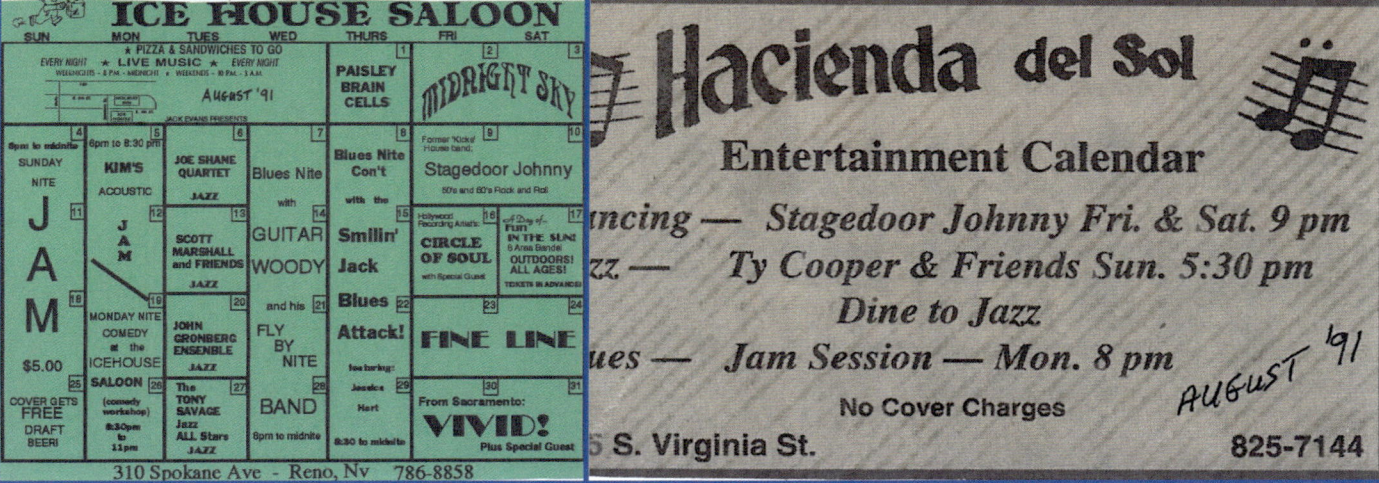

1987

1987

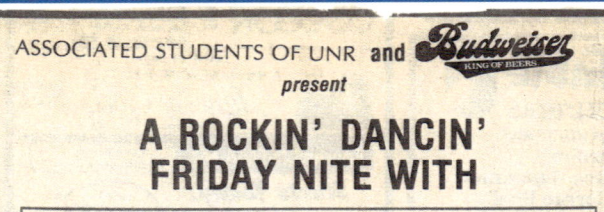

Bob McNamara
1954 - 2023

Crusader Rabbit

Sanchez-Gillette-Loomis Band

INTRODUCING
RazorMaid
HALLOWEEN NITE
ROCTOBER 31 8:00pm

PROMOTIONS
BY
D.J. PURDY

N
W E
S

345 N S

ST. RT. 17

MT ROSE HWY

345 S

GRANGE
HALL

's

$5.00 donation at door

THE
GRAND BALLROOM
Molly Hatchet
Sept. 15 1987

WORKING
PERSONNEL

RAZOR MAID

Curtis Mitchell and John Kirk
"RazorMaid"

White Water
By Mike Biselli

Mike Biselli, along with three of his close friends moved into the Cordone (grandfather & grandmother) ranch house at 895 Kietze Lane (now the Reno Nissan Dealership) in 1976. Shortly after moving in, his girlfriend Karen Rosling (Biselli) was attending a party on 9th Street by UNR where Lee Miles was playing acoustic guitar. Karen told Lee he should meet her boyfriend who plays drums. Karen gave Mike's phone number to Lee and the two of them met at the Kietzke Lane party house. Lee's best friend, guitarist Bob Rasner (RIP) and bass player Ron Coder were asked if they would like to join forces and Revolver was formed. After the family wine cellar was converted into a rehearsal studio, the four got to work spending many hours learning cover songs and writing original music.

The band's first show was a battle of the bands at the Livestock Events Center in Reno with all proceeds benefitting a local food pantry. That show started a long tradition of giving back to the community through volunteering and organizing nonprofit organization benefit shows. Guitarist and singer Gary Fritz joined the band in 1977 as Revolver was playing southern rock and blues. Not long after playing their first show, the band met Mike Mantor and was now represented by Head First Productions! Bass player Steve Funk eventually replaced Ron Coder. Nigel Giddings was added on keyboards and vocals, and joined the band that now became White Water. From the very beginning, the band was very fortunate to have sound engineer Kirk Berryman as well as electrical engineer and equipment manager Mike Goss assisting. Lead singer and Bass player Michael Kelley joined the band in 1979. With the addition of Michael Kelley, the band opened for Cold Blood at the Reindeer Lodge. Eventually keyboard player Todd Silva (RIP) and saxophone player Rick "Heavy" Levy came on board.

It was during the early to mid-1980's that the band was having great success as Mike Mantor was booking shows at the top venues and incredible private parties. With the departure of Todd Silva and Rick Levy, Elise Weatherly joined the band to add keyboards and vocals. In 1986, while playing at Del Mar Station, Robert Foreman approached the band to let them know he was opening Granny's House Recording Studio and that he liked the original material, suggesting the band come over and record at his new studio. Mr. Foreman let the band know they can come and record for $25 dollars per hour so he could get his new recording engineer, Mr. Don Evans, some experience with the new studio. The plan was to record two original songs, but with Don Evans having a great time and learning so much about the new studio, he asked owner Robert Foreman if the band could continue recording at $25 per hour, Mr. Foreman agreed, and the band recorded a total of five original songs.

White Water was the first band to record, produce and release a vinyl EP at Granny's House Recording Studio that was released on MCF Records, owned by Reno icon, Mark Francovich. The art for the album cover was provided by local Sparks artist Greg Flowers. The entire production was financed by Reno Dentist, Dr. Joseph Peri. The EP was submitted to record companies with two record deals offered. White Water also recorded several songs at Starsound Audio recording studios in the mid-1980s.

In 1986, White Water also planned and organized the "For the Love of Lisa" benefit concert to raise the tuition money for "Reno Miracle Girl" Lisa Worobey to attend the Fashion Institute in San Francisco, California. With $15,000 needed to be raised in one night, B.J. Thomas, who had taken Roger Miller's place due to strep throat, was asked to team up with White Water to pack out the Sparks Recreation Center. Mr. Thomas graciously agreed and White Water humbly opened the show and provided him and his band all the musical gear and sound system. After the event, B.J. said he forgot how fun it was to play with people dancing only feet away. This was an unforgettable event that changed the life of not only Lisa, but her entire family! Mr. Thomas was as sweet in person as is voice sounds on his records! With young families to raise and careers taking off, White Water made the decision to stop pursuing a record contract and the band dissolved in 1987.

Members have come and gone, but White Water carries on to this day. The band, as always, is very community-oriented and continues to perform for charitable causes whenever called upon to contribute their talents.

Author's note: Even though White Water, and the band members, were included in the list of bands in our first book, Rock 'n' Reno, there were no photos, posters, etc., due to miscommunication. We have decided that due to that omission, White Water deserves a prominent place in this sequel.

Note from co-author Gerry McCarroll: I worked for the City of Sparks for 21 years and knew both Mike Biselli and Lee Miles. I was not aware that they were local "rock stars"! Little did I know that all these years later I would be writing about them and their band!

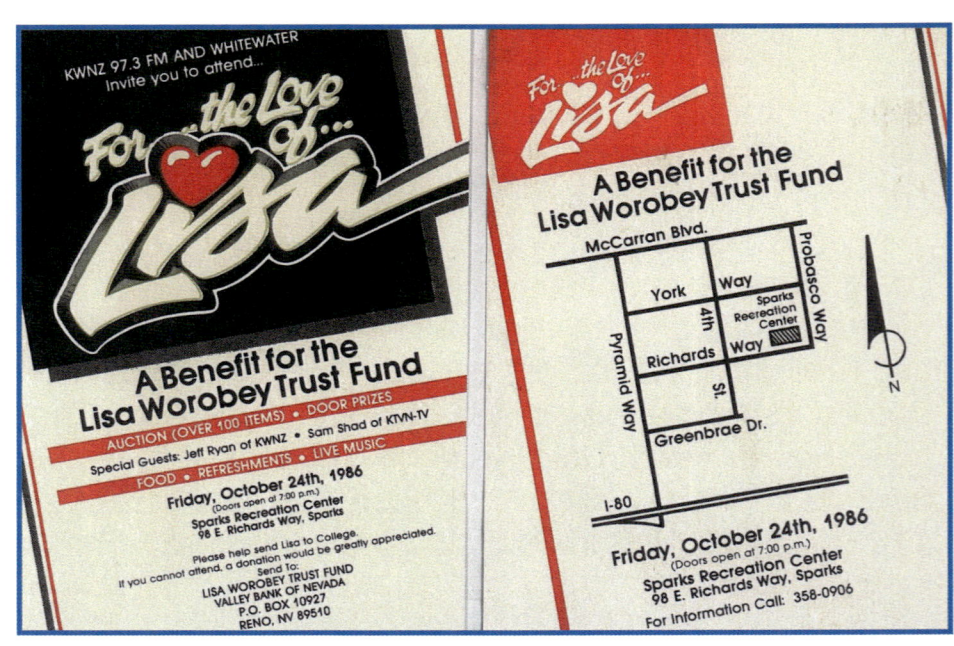

White Water

Starsound Audio Inc.
2679 ODDIE BOULEVARD RENO, NEVADA 89512
(702) 331-1010

March 12, 1986

To whom it may concern,

Mike Biselli (Whitewater) has been doing business with Starsound Audio Inc. for 6 years. They have usually been a prepaid customer which is highly unusual in this line of business. They currently have an open account and make payments on or before the due date.

Mike has always operated in a businesslike manner and is a pleasure to work with.

If you have any questions please feel free to contact me personally.

Scott Bergstrom
President
Starsound Audio Inc.

State of Nevada
A PROCLAMATION
By the Governor

WHEREAS, LISA WOROBEY HAS SPENT THE PAST 7 YEARS OF HER LIFE IN AND OUT OF HOSPITALS, UNDERGOING MAJOR SURGERY, AND FOLLOWING SURGERY IN JANUARY OF THIS YEAR, WAS TOLD SHE HAD ONLY A COUPLE OF WEEKS TO LIVE; AND

WHEREAS, LISA WOROBEY WASN'T READY TO GIVE UP HER LIFE; SHE IS A FIGHTER WHO HAS NEVER LET ILLNESS OR PAIN STOP HER FROM REACHING HER GOALS, AND SHE HAD TOO MANY GOALS YET TO MEET--GRADUATION FROM WOOSTER HIGH SCHOOL, BEING HOME FOR MOTHER'S DAY, AND ATTENDING THE FASHION INSTITUTE OF DESIGN AND MERCHANDISING IN SAN FRANCISCO; AND

WHEREAS, LISA WOROBEY GRADUATED FROM WOOSTER HIGH SCHOOL AT A SPECIAL IN-HOSPITAL COMMENCEMENT CEREMONY SPONSORED BY MAKE-A-WISH AND ATTENDED BY 200 FELLOW STUDENTS, FRIENDS AND FAMILY, AND SOON AFTER BEGAN A MIRACULOUS RECOVERY WHICH ALLOWED HER TO BE HOME FOR MOTHER'S DAY; AND

WHEREAS, LISA WOROBEY IS KNOWN AS "A LIVING LEGEND, THE MIRACLE GIRL," AN INSPIRATION TO ALL WHO HEAR HER STORY. SHE IS ABLE TO WALK, TALK AND EVEN DRIVE A CAR, AND SPENDS HOURS DESIGNING CLOTHING; AND

WHEREAS, LISA WOROBEY'S CURRENT GOAL IS TO ATTEND THE FASHION INSTITUTE OF DESIGN AND MERCHANDISING IN SAN FRANCISCO, WHICH WILL ENABLE HER TO REACH HER LIFELONG DREAM OF BECOMING A FASHION DESIGNER; AND

WHEREAS, MICHAEL BISELLI AND HIS BAND, WHITE WATER, ARE DONATING THEIR TALENTS AND CO-SPONSORING WITH KWNZ-FM, A DANCE AND AUCTION, "FOR THE LOVE OF LISA," TO HELP MAKE LISA WOROBEY'S DREAM OF GOING TO FASHION SCHOOL A REALITY;

NOW, THEREFORE, I, RICHARD H. BRYAN, GOVERNOR OF THE STATE OF NEVADA, DO HEREBY PROCLAIM OCTOBER 24, 1986, IN NEVADA AS

LISA WOROBEY DAY

In Witness Whereof, I have hereunto set my hand and caused the Great Seal of the State of Nevada to be affixed at the State Capitol in Carson City, this 15th day of October, in the year of Our Lord one thousand nine hundred and eighty 6.

Governor

By the Governor:
Secretary of State

By
Deputy

Thanks for the benefit

Recently, a benefit was given for Lisa Worobey by an excellent local band called White Water, which raised a little more than $11,000 for me in one night.

The benefit, For the Love of Lisa, was a very big success, with the governor and the two mayors there, but some people didn't get the recognition they deserve.

Every member of White Water worked very hard, day after day, trying to get donations for the auction, which took a lot of time out of their lives. There were also a lot of people who are not in the band, but donated their time to help at the benefit and make it a success.

There are so many people to personally thank that I could be here forever, so I want everyone to know that I am very grateful to you for making my dream come true — to attend fashion school.

I would really like to thank White Water and especially the head of the band, Mike Biselli, and his wife, Karen, for creating this benefit and working so very hard.

I love you all so much, and I'll never forget you.

You all are very special to me. I love you.

Lisa Worobey, Reno
Oct. 31, 1986

PICNIC APPEARANCE. The musical group White Water will appear at the 4th annual Sparks Family Picnic Saturday, July 27 10 a.m. to 3 p.m. at Ardmore Park at 12th and Oddie. Donation is $2 which includes a meal and prize drawings. Donations benefit Police Widows and Orphans Fund.

TRIBUNE/Ruth Mills

LIVE MUSIC. White Water, a local rock group, entertains the crowd attending the recent Sparks Festival Days at the Iron Horse Shopping Center. The four-piece band performs in the Reno-Carson area.

David Strelz

Kenny Laursen

By LISA LAREE

What are the special qualities that come together to create a figure in contemporary music?

Talent? Yes, to be sure.

Experience and determination? Without a doubt.

But even more important are the intangibles — the spirit and the soul which distinguish dynamic talents from journeyman performers.

KENNY LAURSEN is a singer, a comedian, an impressionist.

Kenny Laursen

The world's tallest elf, and Saudi Arabia's "Most Popular Entertainer of 1976." What more could anyone want, for goshsakes? Maybe some '50s music, wry patter and warm personality? OK, you got it, kiddo. Fitzgerald's lounge through Feb. 5.

Kenny Laursen

It is those qualities which set **Kenny Laursen** apart. More than just a singer, musician, comedian, impressionist, songwriter, **Kenny** is an entertainer.

Six foot, six inches Larsen, was born in Florence, California in November, 1942. Began studing piano at five, played steel guitar and was a virtuoso tuba player at fourteen. His first band was a German polka band, and later switched to Dixieland. In 1959, he created the "World's Only Masked Band", The Phantoms. With that group he played bass for most of the Rock and Roll stars of the period including the Coasters, Fats Domino, Eddie Cochran, Richie Valens, The Olympics, Jerry Lee Lewis, Bobby Day, and many others. This is the secret behind knowing every "Oldie but Goodie", except seven, between the years 1954 to 1961.

Trying to 21 at age 16, Kenny went to Tucson, Arizona to work in one of the roughest night clubs in the country, then six months later found himself in Las Vegas with a group and the number one hit record of the nation, "Lets Think About Livin".

After ten more years of knocking around with a dozen groups all over the county, the Bahamas, and Alaska, Kenny decided to learn the guitar and become a single performer. In five years, he has grown to be one of the most versatile, popular, highest demanded solo entertainers in the industry. Kenny does lots of impressions, Gabby Hayes, John Wayne, Johnny Cash, Truman Capote, John Barrymore, and more. Kenny Laursen's a star you won't want to miss seeing.

Kenny Laursen returned in January from his second series of concerts in Saudi Arabia where he entertained the many thousands of Americans who work for the Aramco Oil Company in that country.

As a result of his first series of concerts in February, 1976, Kenny was voted "Saudia Arabia's Most Popular Entertainer of 1976."

Laursen works with intensity. He is a magnet on stage and his razor-sharp humor sparkles. He loves doing impressions of famous people and just a few are: John Wayne, Gabby Hayes, Bela Lugosi, Liberace, W.C. Fields, Truman Capote and Johnny Cash.

KENNY LAURSEN

The Kenny Laursen Show
Kenny and the Cruisers

KENNY & THE CRUISERS

Metal message

Marilyn Newton/Gazette-Journal

SHOWTIME: Rawkon heavy-metal band members Mikel Grover, left, Marc Grover, center, lead singer, and Harold "Hair-long" Crook perform recently at Wooster High School as part of their campaign against drinking and drugs.

Reno rockers urging teens to party smart

By Mark Fenske

Some people think drugs, partying and drunkenness go hand-in-hand with heavy-metal rock music.

But at least one heavy-metal Reno band plays a different tune. Rawkon delivers the message "don't drink and drive" during concerts promoting Safe Ride.

A privately sponsored organization, Safe Ride offers free transportation on Friday and Saturday nights to teens who have had too much to drink, or who are afraid to ride with someone who has been drinking.

The local heavy-metalers just finished a tour of Reno/Sparks-area high schools to get the message across through a combination of safe-thinking

> ❝ We have a stance of pro-intelligence — everybody's got the choice to kill themselves with drugs, but we choose not to. ❞
>
> **Marc Grover/Rawkon**

rhetoric and rock 'n' roll music.

The Safe Ride benefit tour finale for Rawkon is at the Grand Ballroom on Oct. 21, which Grand Ballroom manager Joel Huntsman said is important to his business. "Being a house that sells alcohol, we've had to become more responsible and hopefully they'll (Rawkon) save a life."

Although their primary emphasis is anti-drinking and driving, Rawkon also takes a stance against drug abuse.

"Everybody likes to have a good time, but our philosophy is to not make it more important than life itself," said Marc Grover, lead singer of Rawkon,

during a break from their seven-show tour.

"We have a stance of pro-intelligence — everybody's got the choice to kill themselves with drugs, but we choose not to."

The idea of using a rock band to discourage high school students from drinking and driving was the brainchild of Safe Ride Promotional Director Kyra Souza.

"In order to get the attention of kids, we had to use something they could relate to," said Souza. "We wanted to let them know that we are the intelligent alternative to getting into a car drunk and hurting someone."

Souza said the purpose of Rawkon's tour is to not only increase awareness of Safe Ride to teens, but to increase the number of volunteers on the Safe Ride staff. Since the Safe Ride tour started, use of the program has increased to about 30 teens per night.

About 90 more adult and 75 teen volunteers are needed for the program, Souza said. Each volunteer works one night approximately every eight weeks.

See METAL, page 10D

Metal music

From page 1D

"We want to see you back, rockin' with us, so don't drink and drive," said Grover from above a sea of young heavy-metal enthusiasts at a recent Wooster High School concert.

It was a show much like the others have been — played in front of a few hundred students during a lunch hour. The crowd was composed mostly of heavy-metal enthusiasts but also had the usual high school stratification ranging from jocks to punk rockers. But more importantly, all who attended received the same message.

Don't drink and drive.

"When your school principal tells you not to drink and drive, stupid'," said 23-year-old Marc Grover, who sports shoulder-length brown hair. "We've lost too many friends to the stupidity of drugs."

Since the release of their debut cassette last August, more than 600 of the $4.95 cassette tapes have been sold.

Much of Rawkon's success has been boosted by the backing of local radio stations, record stores and nightclubs.

KRZQ Station Manager Daniel Cook said Rawkon has a loyal local following and gets regular play on his station.

Rico Imone, assistant manager of U R What U Play Discs and Tapes store, contended that Rawkon has been the most successful local band ever. "Their tapes sold like wildfire when they first came out in August."

nobody listens. But when these guys tell you, people listen," said Brent Wright, 15, a Wooster High sophomore.

"They have an image of being real partiers," said Chris Johnson, 15, another Wooster sophomore. "But then they say something different — 'be careful.' "

Besides the support of the students in attendance, faculty also backed the event.

"It's the kind of music kids like to hear," said Marlys Holman, an English and chorus teacher at Wooster. "It certainly wouldn't do a symphony orchestra any good to relate this message.

"This is their kind of music, just like Bill Haley was mine."

On stage, Grover, 23, is joined by fellow spandex-clad band members Harold "Hairlong" Crook, 20, on lead guitar; Mikel

Several other local record stores carry the tape as well, including The Wherehouse, Mirabelli's, Music City and Budget Tapes and Records.

Despite the backing of several community members, the band's attempt at success has been an arduous one. In order to put out their only tape, the band had to come up with $2,500 for recording and production.

Dave Hoefer, a friend of the band's whom they call their "driving force," came up with 75 percent of the final cost.

"We've got a good thing going and I want to keep it going and get us signed," said Hoefer, referring to the band's aspirations of gaining a recording contract.

Mark Fenske is a free-lance writer and journalism student at the University of Nevada-Reno.

(Mike) Grover (Marc's brother), 20, on bass; Guy "Twin Cannon" Johnson, 28, on drums, and Pete Amato, 20, on keyboards. All are veterans of the teen party scene. And, with the exception of Johnson and Amato, all are alumni of Reno-area high schools.

In addition to anti-drinking and driving advice, the band gives out Safe Ride key chains.

Promoting Safe Ride gives the band more than added recognition, Grover said. It gives them a moral self-satisfaction of aiding in the prevention of a problem that has personally affected every member in the band.

Band members dedicated their first cassette tape, "Rawkon," to the memory of three friends who they say died in drug- and/or alcohol related deaths.

"We woke up and said, 'This is

43

Rawkon

44

Somebody's Kids returns to Del Mar

Reno nightclub Del Mar Station, is open all day and every night, and continually provides the Reno area with a place to go dancing seven nights a week. Live music is performed by popular west coast groups until 3 a.m., Sunday through Thursday, and up until 4 a.m., Friday and Saturday nights.

Tonight through Saturday Del Mar welcomes back the ever requested group that originated right here in Reno, "Somebody's Kids." Since the group formed in 1983, they have been touring the west coast and just recently returned from Guam. "Somebody's Kids" perform danceable Top 40 songs as well as

their own original songs, with style, energy and a certain drive recognized by audiences everywhere they play.

Thursday night coupled with live music by "Somebody's Kids" is KOZZ and Del Mar's annual "Toys for Tots" party. Starting at 9 p.m., bring a toy for an underprivileged child to Del Mar Station, and the cover charge is free. Take the opportunity to feel good about yourself and make somebody's Christmas a happy one. There will be live music and dancing, lots of prizes and giveaways, all night long at Del Mar Station, corner of Virginia St. and St. Lawrence.

Somebody's Kids

DO OR DIE SITUATION

SOMBODYS KIDS

SOMBODYS KIDS

SIDE 1
45 RPM

SBK-2520
SK PRODUCTIONS

"DO OR DIE SITUATION"
(O. Mitchell and Sombodys Kids)

SOMEBODY'S KIDS

Dr. Downs to appear at Del Mar

Open all day and every night, Reno nightclub Del Mar Station features a variety of entertainment weekly.

This week is no exception, starting with Thursday evening, when Dr. Downs, the rock and roll hypnotist debuts at Del Mar Station. Currently touring the U.S., Dr. Downs has been recognized as a perfect act especially when combined with rock and roll audiences.

Sometimes amazing and other times strange, Dr. Downs supplies a good natured performance. Selecting people from the audience as stage subjects, Dr. Downs performs a series of antics which entertain all, hurt no one and at no time prove to be embarrassing to those taking part in the act.

Dr. Downs performs this Thursday night only at Del Mar Station with two shows. The first show begins at 9:30 p.m. and the other at 12:30 a.m.

In addition to his two performances will be live music provided by a hometown favorite Somebody's Kids. Performing Top 40 rock The Kids also do some original material, including Do Or Die Situation off this years KOZZ homegrown album available now at local record stores. Their unique combination of personality, energy and musicianship guarantees a fun-filled danceable evening. They will be appearing at Del Mar through Sunday.

Along with the usual entertainment, two full bars, dancing and a complete pool and game room, the Del Mar Deli will also be open Relax and enjoy Moms home cooking every day for lunch and daily until 1 a.m.

Gold Watch
and a Chain

SOMBODYSKIDS

ROCK BLVD.

Gilbert Trujillo

Gilbert has been a fixture on the Reno music scene for over 50 years. He has been an integral part of several of Reno's most popular rock bands.

Now a pediatric dentist of note, he still gets the itch to break out the guitar on occasion and revisit his rock 'n' roll roots with some of our local bands.

Provide music

Gilbert Trujio, left, and Bryon Jackson provided music for the second annual summer dance sponsored by the Ormsby Association for Retarded Children held recently at the Governor's Mansion.

TAXI

THE TOUCH

EUROTOUCH

Eurotouch

Scratch

New Year's Eve

Midnight Balloon Drop!

Party!

Tommy Bell, Reno's Entertainer of the Year, rings in the New Year at our non-stop party. Join us for cake, champagne and a balloon drop on the casino floor at midnight.

AT THE PEPPERMILL: Graveyard king Tommy Bell will be rocking the masses through Jan. 8. Bell is a favorite among local musicians and is one of the area's finest.

Curt Mitchell, Reno guitarist, far right. Formerly of "Somebody's Kids".

1992

ON TARGET

Dave Campanaro

The music of Paul McCartney, as performed by Dave Campanaro, will fill the Eldorado's cabaret April 16-21. "Let it Be," "Live and Let Die," "Long and Winding Road," "Band on the Run" and "Penny Lane" are just a sample of the titles Campanaro will perform.

Since the age of 6, friends, relatives and even total strangers have told Campanaro "you look just like Paul McCartney." After joining a band in Buffalo and then moving on to play Los Angeles nightclubs in the late '70s, he finally decided to take advantage of this comparison, and in 1980 he formed "Penny lane—A Tribute to The Beatles." Determined to make Penny Lane the most genuine Beatles tribute ever, Campanaro bought a vintage Hoffner Beatle bass, wore the grooves out of his old Beatle records and studied endless McCartney concert footage to imitate his facial expressions and mannerisms.

For more than a decade, he has been exciting audiences with his tribute to McCartney, including viewers of "PM Magazine" and "Geraldo." He has performed in more than 400 sold-out shows with the acclaimed "Legends in Concert."

Band on the Run

Band on the Run

Dave Campanaro with Paul Revere

FUN & GAMING

Vol. 21 ... Jan. 4, 198...

DAVE CAMPANARO
A TRIBUTE TO
PAUL McCARTNEY
DEC. 23 - JAN. 1

ROB HANNA
A SALUTE TO
ROD STEWART
DEC. 26 - JAN. 15

ELDORADO
HOTEL CASINO
RENO

"Paul" and "Rod"

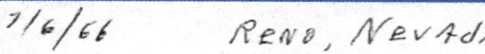
7/6/66 RENO, NEVADA

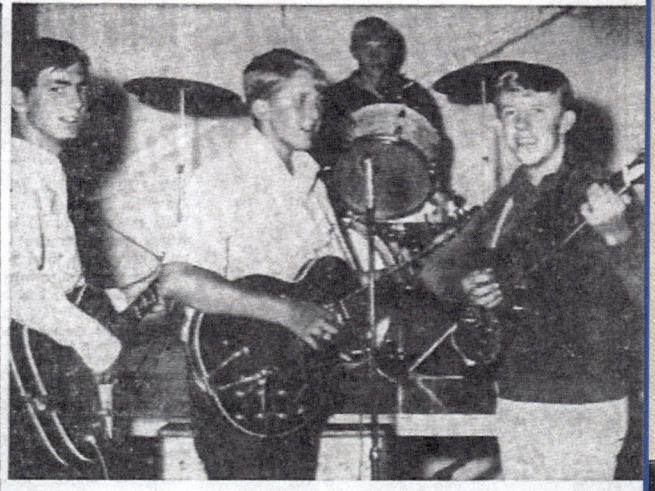

'The Undecided'

Ralph Henson, Bob Place, Ron Franklin, Richard Henderson, from left, with Bob Daly, not shown, will furnish the live music for the Thursday dances at the YWCA for junior high school-age young people. The supervised dances will be held from 7 to 9:30 p.m. (White Photo)

BAND OF THE WEEK – ENTERTAINING TEENAGERS Saturday at the Civic Auditorium from 8 to 11:30 p.m. will be "The Monarchs" pictured above. School dress for the dance, open to persons between the ages of 13 and 18, is required. The dance is sponsored by the Carson City Recreation Dept.

DANCE TO THE MUSIC OF

THE MONARCHS

AT

CHIPS CELLAR   9TH AND VIRGINIA

ADMISSION		DOORS OPEN
$1.00 STAG	************	8.30
$1.50 DRAG	************	FRIDAY NIGHT

Precious Metal

RAYGE

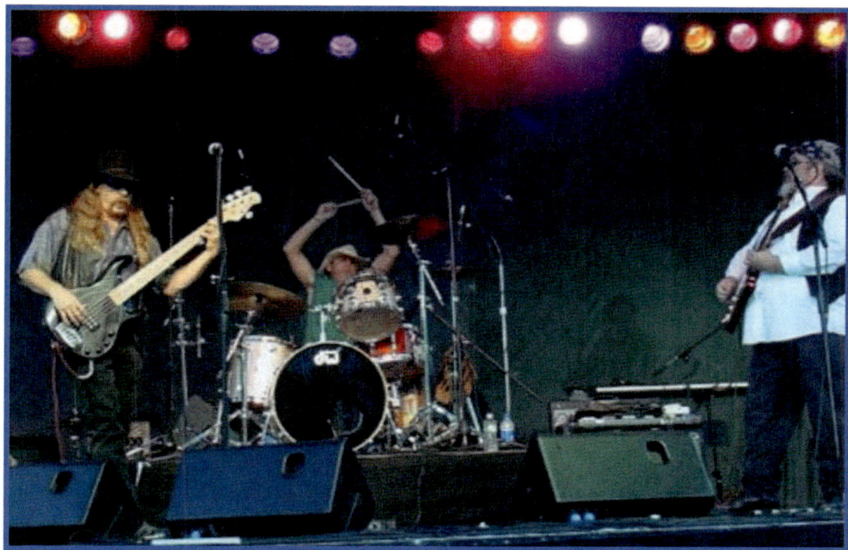

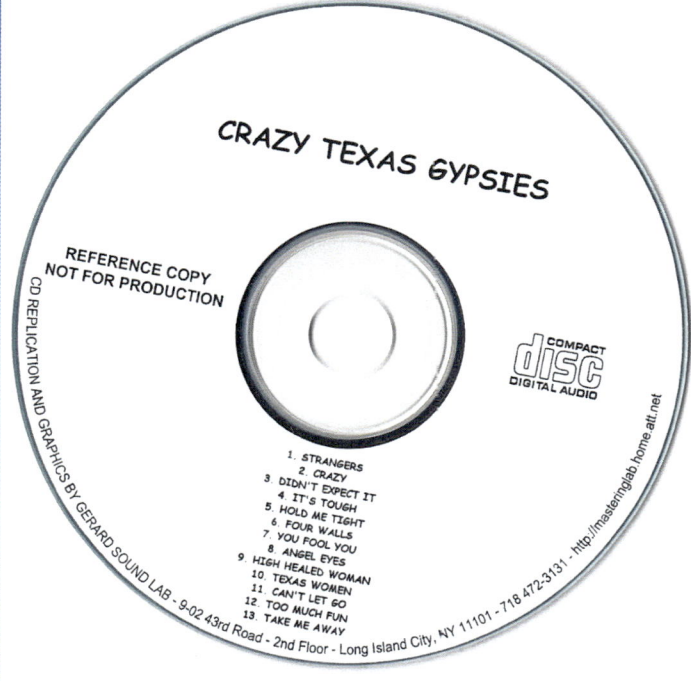

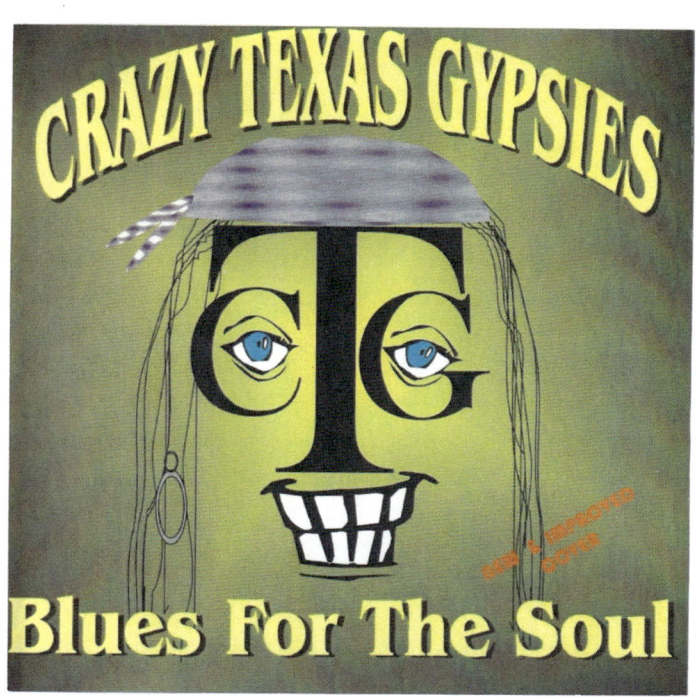

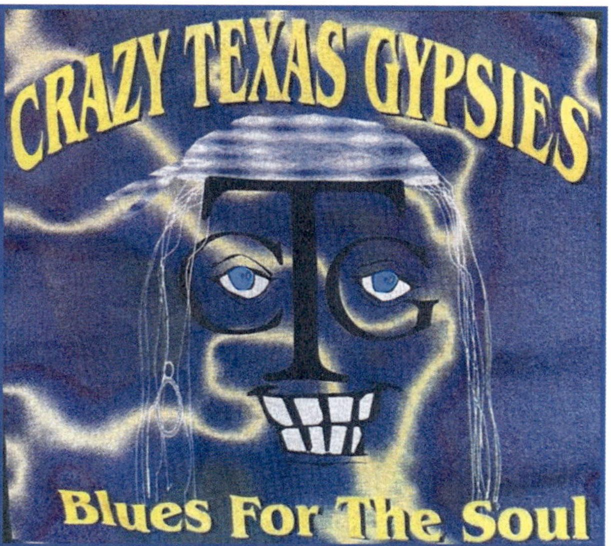
CRAZY TEXAS GYPSIES
CTG
Blues For The Soul

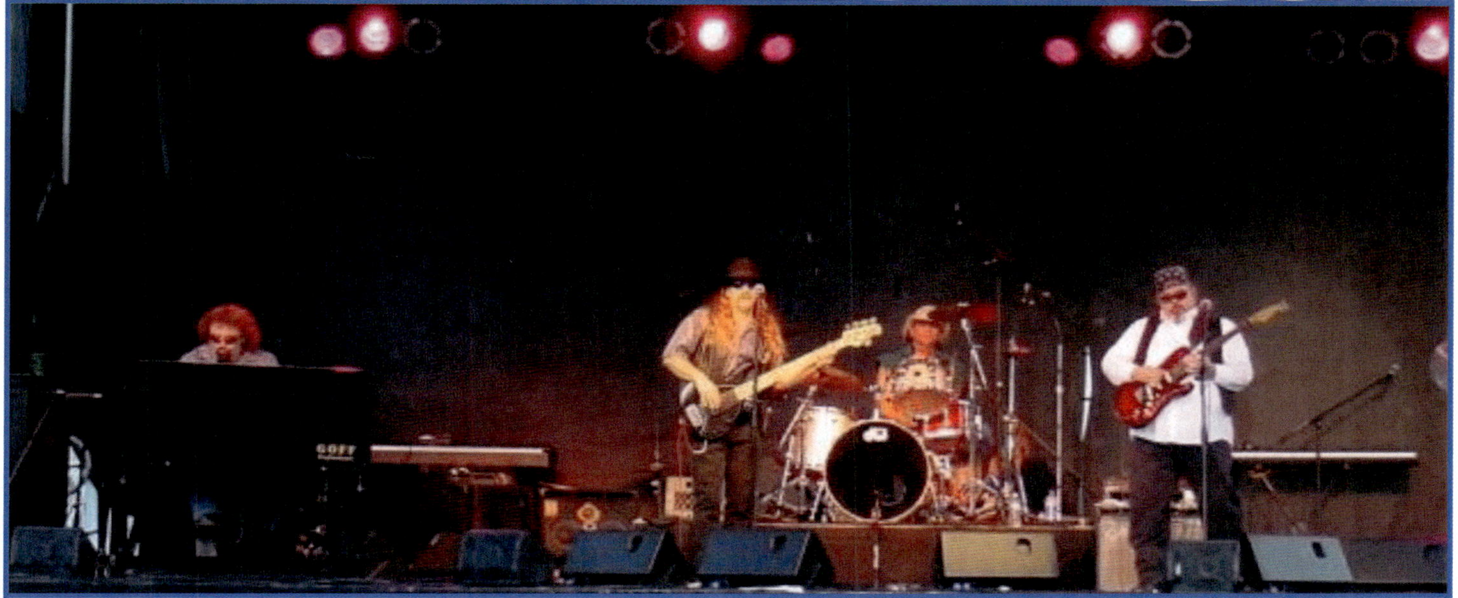

CRAZY TEXAS GYPSIES
REFERENCE COPY
NOT FOR PRODUCTION
COMPACT disc DIGITAL AUDIO
1. STRANGERS
2. CRAZY
3. DIDN'T EXPECT IT
4. IT'S TOUGH
5. HOLD ME TIGHT
6. FOUR WALLS
7. YOU FOOL YOU
8. ANGEL EYES
9. HIGH HEALED WOMAN
10. TEXAS WOMEN
11. CAN'T LET GO
12. TOO MUCH FUN
13. TAKE ME AWAY
CD REPLICATION AND GRAPHICS BY GERARD SOUND LAB - 9-02 43rd Road - 2nd Floor - Long Island City, NY 11101 - 718 472-3131 - http://masteringlab.home.att.net

CRAZY TEXAS GYPSIES
CTG
Blues For The Soul

John Sanchez—Chuck Ruff Group
1976

When Gary Met Sandy
By Gerry Foster McCarroll

A Reno-Tahoe staple of nighttime entertainment during the late 70's, and into the 80's and 90's was the duo "Gary & Sandy", aka "Gary & Sandy's Common Ground". (Gary Raffanelli and Sandy Selby). Many an enjoyable evening was spent by locals in various casino lounges, listening to both Gary and Sandy singing, and Gary on the keyboard, accompanied by their backup band. They were well-known for their blend of rock and pop, as well as their playful banter onstage. Plus, Gary could really rock that mullet! But how did they meet and get their start? Well, I'll tell you…

Gary grew up in Richmond, California, with sister Karen, and brothers Mike and Dave. From an early age, Gary was fascinated by accordion players he saw on the Mickey Mouse Club. Later, his hero was Dick Contino, the legendary virtuoso of the accordion. At the age of 8 he began taking accordion lessons and, eventually, became adept at also playing the piano, organ, and keyboard. He was 12 when he started his own band, "The Vulcans", and at 14, he joined his brother's band, a group called the "Vandells". They played in the San Francisco area from 1966 to 1970.

Jim Burgett was a well-known singer/performer in the Reno/Tahoe area. In the summer of '64 he started putting on teen dances at the American Legion Hall in South Lake Tahoe. At that same time every summer, Jim would book "The Vandells" at the American Legion Hall. Gary met and impressed Jim with his keyboard skills. The "Vandells" broke up at the beginning of 1970, and Jim lost his band at the same time. He called on Gary to be his keyboard player.

Gary performed with Jim off and on for about 6 months, and on his last night at Harrah's Tahoe, he was inspired when he met the girl and guy duo of "Beverlee and Sidro and the Sneakers", who were regulars in the casino lounge scene in Reno and Tahoe. (Sidro Garcia and Beverlee Brown). In 1971 Gary got a call from Sidro for an audition, which he jumped at. Gary drove to Reno to audition, but Sidro hired his keyboard player back. However, Sidro set up another audition with a band called The Relatives at the Riverside Hotel. Gary passed that audition with one song and worked the entire summer in Portland, Oregon, and Tucson and Phoenix, Arizona.

Back in the Bay Area, Gary formed a group he called "Gary & Friends" in 1972. Remember being inspired by "Beverlee & Sidro"? Well, he hired a girl singer named Michelle, and renamed the group "Gary & Chelle". Things went well for a while, but tensions began to occur between Michelle and others in the band. After a particularly raucous rehearsal, Michelle unceremoniously quit the band. And so, Gary began the quest for a new female "partner".

ne quest was not without its ups and downs. Gary learned of a female singer who was young, green, and inexperienced She was 18 and just out of high school. Gary got a call from the girl's parents who were concerned about her naivete and getting involved in a band with a bunch of musicians. A parent's worst nightmare, apparently! Gary assured them that he didn't drink or do drugs and would watch over her. As rehearsals began, it was apparent that indeed, the girl was green and inexperienced, and she soon left the band. That experiment ended and the uphill battle to find a suitable female singer began again.

The band went back to "Gary & Friends", from "Gary & Chelle", and they were working regularly, but Gary still wanted a better female singer. He found a girl named Paula C. from Sacramento. She didn't have the look he wanted, nor the voice, but she was a girl, and fit at least one of his criteria, so he hired her. The arrangement lasted for 3 months, but it wasn't ideal. At the end of her contract, on New Year's Eve, she left the band, and he never heard from her again.

Disheartened, Gary almost gave up looking for a female singer. In January 1973, he got a call from an agent who wanted to hire a band to replace a Mariachi band at a Mexican restaurant/bar in Concord, California. Gary cobbled together a group with his brother Dave and one of his old bandmates from the "Vandells". Within a month they became so popular that the restaurant was packed every night that they played. Even with that resurgence to his career, he still wanted to hire a girl singer. His fortune and future were about to change forever.

Gary, 1973

On one of his regular visits to his favorite music store, he mentioned to the owner, Tony Scalise, that he wanted to hire another girl singer. Tony told Gary that his guitar teacher had a music student who was a police officer who worked for the Kensington Police Department under Chief Walter Gist, who had a daughter by the name of Sandy Gist who just might fit the bill. Gary asked Tony to give his number to the police officer. Little did he know that he had just been handed the golden ticket!

He called Sandy and that same night she and her mother came to the restaurant to see the show. They met during the break. Even early on, there was a chemistry between them.

Sandy Gist

The next day Gary invited Sandy to the Contra Costa Music Department, because he wanted to hear her sing. In a private music room, Sandy began singing for Gary. He told her right away that, because she was singing in a falsetto, operatic voice, that it wasn't what he was looking for, and that he wanted more ROCK sound. He asked her if she knew "Proud Mary". She took to the challenge, and Gary knew he had found what he was looking for. He was about to fulfill his dream that had been inspired by "Sidro and Beverlee".

He had found his Beverlee! There were a few roadblocks along the way, i.e., a club manager refusing to pay Sandy to sing on stage, so Gary left that job and secured another job in Seattle. Sandy was now touring with "Gary & Friends".

Sandy eventually changed her last name from Gist to Selby, her grandmother's maiden name, and "Gary & Friends" became "Gary & Sandy's Common Ground". Gary was attracted to Sandy from the first time that they met, but he kept his distance from a romantic relationship. From experience he knew that mixing business and pleasure didn't always work out well, so he kept his distance...for a while. Then, there was the kiss...

"Gary & Sandy" toured from 1973 to 1975. They wanted to come to Reno to perform, especially at Harrah's. They contacted Jim Thompson, who was the entertainment director at the Sparks Nugget. After a quick meeting with Jim and Jim's friend Bobby Dee, they hired Bobby Dee as their manager. They began officially working in Reno on July 4, 1976, making it their new hometown.

Their bookings took them to, among others, the Cal-Neva Lodge, the Tahoe Biltmore, Fitzgerald's, Harvey's, and their biggest and most successful contract, the MGM, aka Bally's. Harrah's Reno/Tahoe hired them from the MGM in 1985-86.

The group's name changed over time from "Gary & Friends" in 1973, to "Gary's Common Ground" from 1974 to 1976, to "Gary & Sandy's Common Ground" in 1976, to "Gary & Sandy", and even for a short time to "Raffanelli & Selby", to "Gary Raffanelli & Sandy Selby", finally ending with their full names.

And the kiss? Well, they were a couple for a while, but the mixing of business and pleasure just didn't work out, so they became good friends, which they remain to this day.

They continued on to have the longest running contract at the MGM. In 19 years, they recorded 4 albums and were on over 30 magazine covers, appearing on the first cover on Fun & Gaming Magazine. They toured constantly until October 2004.

(Gary) Raffanelli & Sandy Selby

They autographed this photo for me years ago.

FUN & GAMING

ALADDIN

GARY & SANDY

FUN & GAMING

The Legend of...
Sir Raffanelli & Lady Selby
EXCALIBUR

FUN & GAMING

Gary & Sandy
IN CONCERT
MGM GRAND HOTEL
RENO
NEVADA

FUN & GAMING

Gary & Sandy

ELDORADO
HOTEL • CASINO

GARY & SANDY'S COMMON GROUND

1977

GARY AND SANDY share common ground. In fact, that's the name of their act, which is playing in the lounge of the Cal-Neva Lodge at Crystal Bay through Sept. 17. After Gary and Sandy's engagement, the Cal-Neva's lounge will boast the Jerry Sun Show, opening Sept. 19.

Reno-Lake Tahoe/February 9-15

Entertainment

Reno Gazette-Journal
Advertising Section

GARY & SANDY

At the MGM
See page 4

Plus complete entertainment, skiing, dining and gaming information inside

Nevada Playwor

HARRAH'S RENO CASINO CABARET NEXT FOR GARY & SANDY
Northeast Bay singers rapidly climbing Silver Circuit ladder

Gary & Sandy's star may become brighter

By BILL BOYER

Last week, in the 24th floor penthouse of Harrah's Reno hotel, singers Gary & Sandy arrived on time for their afternoon appointment with the personal manager of Frank Sinatra, Jilly Rizzo.

The two sat nervously as Rizzo bounced from desk to desk answering phone calls. At one point Sinatra Himself strode leisurely past dressed in yellow golfing togs. The phones eventually let up and Rizzo confronted the two. "To be perfectly honest. . ." he began in his Wolfman Jack-like voice.

Gary & Sandy sagged, recalling their performance on Harrah's lounge stage the previous day. The mikes were too low, the sound was bad and the cleaners had mis-shaped Sandy's dress to the point where two safety pins were needed to tuck in the waist. Those were the highlights.

Rizzo continued, "To be perfectly honest, I like you kids."

Gary & Sandy eagerly leaned forward.

"No," added Rizzo as G & S sagged, "I like you kids a lot!"

Bobbing like corks in water, G & S surfaced for the last time as Rizzo promised to "light a fire" under them in Las Vegas.

Their meeting with Rizzo could be the break they've been waiting for ever since they left the Bay Area for the Reno-Tahoe-Las Vegas Silver Circuit two years ago. Gary Raffanelli grew up in Richmond, Sandy Selby in Kensington. Reno has been their base since 1976.

Gary & Sandy were back in the Bay Area earlier this week and related the above story over breakfast at Kirby's El Cerrito Station. They were bubbling with enthusiasm and confidence.

Ten days ago they had played Harrah's Tahoe and, according to Gary, "it's the best it's ever gone." The quintet, billed as Gary & Sandy's Common Ground, appear in Harrah's Casino Cabaret in Reno Aug. 7-8 and 14-15, play Tommy Lee's Islander in Stockton Aug. 17-27 and return to headline Cal Neva at North Shore for three weeks beginning Aug. 29.

They also have an album out called "That Makes Two of Us". It was written by Jerry Fuller, who has also produced albums for Mac Davis, Johnny Mathis and Glen Campbell.

Both sing and play keyboard. Gary's vocalizing leans on the style of Mac Davis and Kenny Rogers, while Sandy gushes energy, honesty and charisma in her vocal offerings. Two years ago she was named top female lounge singer in Nevada by Entertainment magazine. They blend country, pop, rock and nostalgic tunes in their act.

G & S's meeting with Rizzo came about by accident. They normally make it a practice to introduce themselves to the top-name entertainers who pass through Reno and, after shaking hands with Red Skelton, Gloria Loring and Ronnie Schell, they tried calling on Sinatra. They left a half-dozen messages for Rizzo and five minutes after the last try, he called back.

They met with him that evening and were invited to Sinatra's rehearsal the next day. They found the fabled singer dressed in an orange T-shirt that read "Gossip Writers Stink", orange-tinted sunglasses and a baseball cap.

Sinatra couldn't make their special performance, but Rizzo and other members of his troupe, in addition to Loring and Schell were present.

"With all the problems we figured we blew it," said Gary, overlooking basic fact that a bad sound system and safety pins can not hide real talent.

Gary singing to his Dad

GARY & SANDY
from clay to crystal

That Makes Two Of Us
Gary & Sandy

SAHARA
NOW IN GILDED CAGE LOUNGE
GARY & SANDY
NIGHTLY EXC MON
COMING OCT 3 RUSTY WARREN SHOW

Gary Raffanelli, "Devil With The Blue Dress On", Onstage with "Solid Gold"

Nice legs, Gary!

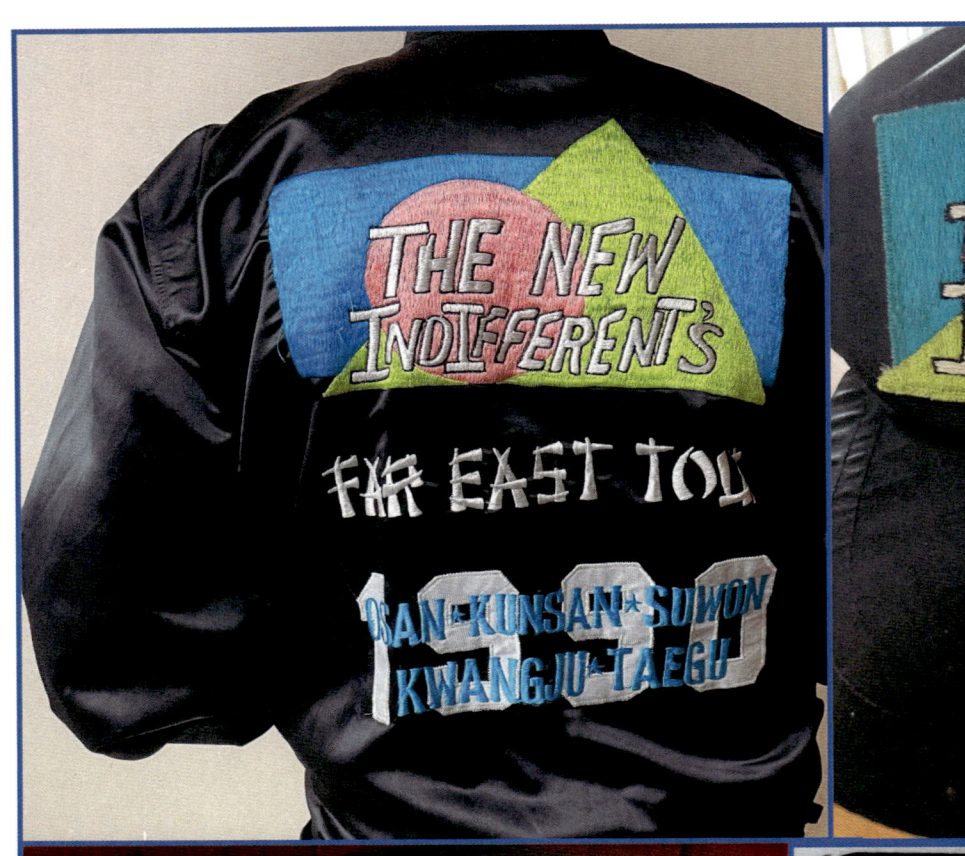

The Jesters Song List handwritten:

Organ Solos

fast	1.)	No Trespassing
fast	2.)	Tuff Turf
medium	3.)	Dawn go away
slow	4.)	Lonely Boy
slow	5.)	Geri
slow	7.)	Our Winter Love
fast	8.)	Hava Nagila
slow	9.)	That Boy
slow	10.)	Blue on Blue
fast	11.)	Jimilou
fast	12.)	Earthquake
slow	13.)	Midsummer's Song
medium	14.)	Death of a Shennins

Others (not played at dances) (organ)

Miserlou
Wild Weekend
Mr. Moto
Penetration
Baja
Out of Limits
Please, Please me
Monzalin
Moon Dawg
Wipe Out
Pipeline
New Girl in School
County Fair
Tra's a Place
Thank you Girl

Jesters Song List 1964

Direct from Lake Tahoe

CRAIG EVANS TRIO

Monday through Thursday
9 p.m. to 2 a.m.
Friday And Saturday
10 p.m. to 3 a.m.

Entertainment and dancing on our STAINLESS STEEL DANCE FLOOR

famous **$3.95**

ONE PRICE STEAK DINNERS
(U.S. CHOICE GRADE)

Surrender tonight … to the thrill of being in BLACK ANGUS COUNTRY

Dedly Biznes

Kirk Poole

Guitar *Woody* & The **Boilers**

KELLY'S BOOGIE BAND

John Mark

KENMARK MUSIC PRODU...
FORREST & QIST BOO... 3 A...
NOLENSVILLE, TENN-...

SH CORRAL
CASINO CABARET
5195 SUN VALLEY DR., SUN VALLEY, NEVADA 89431
Ph 702-673-4477

FEATURING

KELLY'S BOOGIE COUNTRY BAND

WED. THRU SAT.
OPEN 11: A.M. TIL ? DAILY

ONE
FREE DRINK
PER PERSON

2nd Annual
"St Patricks Dance"
Live Music
by Kelly's Boogie Band
RAFFLE!

Drinks .15¢
$2.00 PER PERSON   DOOR PRIZES

DATE- 3-18-78
PLACE- Comstock Rec. Center
TIME- 8:00..... UNTIL ?
SPONSORED BY nevada hi-rollers
4 WHEEL DRIVE CLUB

KELLY'S BOOGIE BAND

KENMARK MUSIC PRODUCTIONS

FUN & GAMING

Glenn
WILLIAMS

The Tahoe Daily Tribune's Entertainment Weekly • Nov. 18-24, 1994

lake tahoe
action
arts & adventure

Park it in the snow
Lots of fun, lots of places, not lots of money

Still hot
Rumors of "Hot, Hot, Hot's" demise were greatly exaggerated

page 9

page 14

Every song you wanted to hear but were afraid to ask.
Glenn Williams and his elaborate repertoire...page 10

Glenn Williams ventures on his own on the Eldorado stage

Glenn Williams, a superb vocalist and musician who has recently teamed up with comedian **Danny Marona**, is venturing out on his own, with Danny's help.

His first solo engagement is booked at the Eldorado Hotel/Casino through March 1.

"Danny's great," Williams said, "because he has given me the opportunity to play with his band on my own.

"It's good for the band, too," he continues, "because it gives them another musical outlet. We do just about everything, with an emphasis on country and '50s and '60s."

Williams favors country music. He says he enjoys singing it and his audiences enjoy hearing it. "There's a great demand for country music from Reno audiences."

Glenn Williams is a vocalist and musician starting on his solo career.

The latest evolution of country music from the twangy, slow sound of the 1970s to the acoustical, upbeat sound of the '90s is what, according to Williams, has cast country music into a new light.

"Today's country music artists are setting a new trend. **Clint Black**, **Randy Travis** and **Garth Brooks** seem to be the most popular," Williams said.

Williams is working on a new album titled "A Little Bit City, a Little Bit Country." It's scheduled for release this spring and will contain original material, as well as popular remakes.

See this up-and-coming, talented, young entertainer nightly at the Eldorado through March 1. Call (800) 648-5966 for more information. Inside Nevada, call 786-5700.

The Eldorado Hotel/Casino is conveniently located on Virginia Street in downtown Reno.

John Von Nolde

For the record

MIXERS: Frenz plays a mix of rhythm and blues and rock 'n' roll dance music.

Popular Reno band Frenz aims at the big time

Frenz. Rhythm and blues, rock 'n' roll dance music. Easy Street, Keystone Shopping Center, 10 p.m. Wednesday through Saturday.

By Marc Picker

Being a hit band in Reno is one thing, but can a group called Frenz make it big nationwide?

That's what the group hopes to do, with the help of Atlantic Records and Keith Olsen, the hottest producer in the business, who recently signed the band to record an album with release tentatively scheduled for spring 1990.

> **❛** We've always been able to break all the rules and still work in casinos. **❜**
>
> **Steven Cowart/Frenz founder**

Despite these heady happenings, this band isn't feeling any pressure. In fact, while waiting to head into the recording studio or take to the road for a concert tour, Frenz will continue to play the Reno-Sparks area rock clubs where they have built a solid following in the past few years with their fast-paced mix of rhythm and blues, rock 'n' roll and dance music.

Until four years ago, Frenz wasn't looking for a recording contract. The band was content to play the casino lounge circuit of Reno-Lake Tahoe-Las Vegas-Atlantic City. That edition of the band played music ranging from jazz to light rock, featured a lot of harmonies, a few dance routines and a lot of shtick.

The current Frenz began to take shape in 1985, when founder-lead guitarist-vocalist Steven Cowart, 36, began hiring new musicians, intending to create a band that would write and record original music, and leave the lounges for the concert stage.

Since then, "We've always been able to break all the rules and still work in casinos," Cowart said during a recent group interview. "In a strange course of events, we became the new standard (in area lounges). The first ones to break the rules become the new standard."

See FRENZ, page 2D

75

Frenz' record

From page 1D

When the band came together, four of the five members were living in Las Vegas. At the beginning of the summer of 1988, Frenz began an indefinite run at Harrah's Reno, and the other members joined keyboardist Jeff Neiman, 31, as Reno-area residents.

The success of this edition of the band, Cowart pointed out, is a tribute to the cohesiveness of its members, with Cowart and Neiman joining Cowart's brother, Doug, 37, who plays bass guitar, Kris Landrum, 27, on synthesizer and drummer Steve Grantham, 30.

Each member of the band brings a distinctive musical background, and that has led Frenz into a unique style that is hard to pin down. Steven Cowart explained that the band has a "dangerous" habit of riding the line between rock 'n' roll and rhythm and blues.

"It's not easy for us to determine where our hearts lie, but this is a business and you have to market your product to the masses. You can't sell Jaguars to a Ford audience, so we're trying to maintain an R&B feel but yet use rock production techniques and attitudes.

"This one record company executive came to see us at Harrah's last year and asked, 'What are you, an R&B band or a rock band?' And my answer was, 'Yes.'"

Fitting Frenz into a specific market may be difficult, but no matter what the audience is finally determined to be, this band is determined to make the most of its shot at the big time. Working with a producer responsible for the sales of 65 million records by artists ranging from Ozzy Osbourne to Whitesnake to Rick Springfield fulfills "a big chunk" of the band's dreams.

"I think this is our chance, and if we don't make it, it is not like 'Tough luck, we didn't make it,'" Neiman said. "To me, it will be like we took our shot. It doesn't mean we'll quit the music business if it's not a success, but I'm not so sure this band will go chasing another recording offer after all this is done if nothing ever comes of it ... This is our shot with THE producer, an we'll take advantage of it."

Landrum agrees. "When I joined the band, I knew that this band would grab these kind of opportunities and kick ass."

"Even if we don't sell 12 million records," Landrum noted, "I don't think it's going to be because we didn't do what we do good. I know we'll do exactly what this band has a magic of doing."

Neiman said producer Olsen "is going to bring out the absolute best that this band has to offer. He's already done that. We sent him a demo with six tunes and felt real good about two of them, but he didn't hesitate to tell us, 'That's two for the album — now let's keep going.' He's going to keep wringing this band until we are giving 150 percent of what we're capable of, and, if we never go any further, then the band couldn't ask for any more."

Frenz' mix of styles, visuality and musical proficiency has earned them a sizable following in Reno, and the band plans to maintain its connections here even after becoming successful. That's a reward to fans here for the attention they've showed the band.

With all this success, Frenz is seeing the fruition of its members' dreams ... dreams that could make a reality of Doug Cowart's joking remark:

"Yeah, we'll be the first supergroup of the '90s."

Marc Picker is a Reno attorney.

IN TIME FOR THE WEEKEND: Frenz, the multi-talented musical ensemble, performs at 10 p.m. Thursday through Saturday at The Great Escape, 1537 S. Virginia Ave. Frenz offers a repertoire of music ranging from the styles of Chicago and Steely Dan to the jazzy funk sounds of today. There is a cover charge. For more information, call 323-1761.

Steel Breeze

You may remember the "You Don't Want Me Anymore" music video and most likely, you've heard the Budweiser jingle they recorded. However, if you want to experience Steel Breeze live, the best place to see the band is the Eldorado through July 16.

Formed in northern California in 1976, Steel Breeze signed with RCA in 1983 and released their first major-label album, "Steel Breeze." Their song "You Don't Want Me Anymore" made it to the Top 10 and the band went on to perform with Hall & Oates, The Who and Huey Lewis and The News.

Spike Orberg
"Steel Breeze"

Steel Breeze blows strong through many changes

By Neil Baron

Evolution of a lounge act:

■ A party band from UC-Davis in California is formed in 1976. They call themselves Steel Breeze.

■ From 1976 through 1983, Steel Breeze develops a name in local nightclubs and pubs. The band goes through 32 different musicians.

■ The band signs with RCA in 1983 and releases their first major label album called "Steel Breeze." Their song "You Don't Want Me Anymore" cracks the top 10 on national charts. Only keyboardist Rod Toner remains from the original 1976 version.

■ Steel Breeze performs live in front of more than 1 million people in 1983. Included are 32 dates opening for Daryl Hall and John Oates. Steel Breeze also performs with The Who, Kansas, Jefferson Starship, Huey Lewis & The News, Berlin, Cheap Trick, Santana and many others. A music magazine calls Steel Breeze the seventh best new act of 1983, behind such names as U2, Duran Duran and Flock of Seagulls.

■ A second song, "Dreamin' is Easy," reaches the top 30.

■ The release of a second album in 1984 is

> *"We're not living off our past We don't have enough of a past to live off of."*
> **Steel Breeze keyboardist Rod Toner**

canned because of what Toner calls "a shady production company."

■ With no new material on the record store shelves, Steel Breeze fades from the national scene.

■ By 1987, everyone involved with the band's first album is gone, except Toner. Three new musicians are recruited and Steel Breeze, in essence, starts over again, playing fairs and nightclubs in northern California and casinos in northern Nevada.

■ The band releases their second album, "Cry Thunder," in 1989 on a small independent label. A third album, "Still Warriors," is cut in 1992.

■ By 1994, Steel Breeze is one of the most popular lounge acts in northern Nevada, continually bringing in large crowds by casino standards.

You might think that watching his band slip from national prominence to a casino lounge act would be a major disappointment for Toner. But he doesn't see it that way.

"We had a lot of great moments and made a lot of money," he said. "I can't complain. For every band that's had as much success as Steel Breeze, there's 10,000 bands that would like to have reached the level we did."

Toner is an optimist. His present band, consisting of singer-songwriter-bassist Bob Thompson, guitarist Rob Bickford and drummer Paul Ojeda, have been together for seven years. They added local singer Kat Wilson, formerly of Vamp, on vocals for 1994.

Steel Breeze has just completed their fourth album, "Peace of Mind," and is looking for a label in the United States. The music is more adult-contemporary compared to the pop rock sound that made Steel Breeze popular in the '80s. Toner believes this album can bring Steel Breeze back onto the charts.

"I still feel the best is ahead of us," he said. "Rob and Bob are 32 and are just beginning to create and apply themselves as professionals. They're very young and aggressive. I believe in this band."

Toner knows that the chances of going from stardom to relative obscurity and back to stardom are slim. But he said he's proud of what this band is accomplishing.

Steel Breeze

"We're not living off our past," he said. "We don't have enough of a past to live off of."

About 30 percent of Steel Breeze's live show is dedicated to original material. The rest are covers of bands ranging from Sly and the Family Stone to Aretha Franklin to Credence Clearwater Revival to slivers of Black Sabbath. And they play a sizzling version of Lynyrd Skynyrd's "Free Bird."

"We've always gone against the normal stock cabaret lounge act," Toner said. "We still think we can kick it really hard. We try to adapt to the house (casino) we're playing in."

While Steel Breeze has lost their visibility, they haven't lost their talent or the ability to produce high-quality professional music.

Steel Breeze may never have another chart-breaking single but for what they are now, a lounge act, they're simply at the top of the heap.

Elsewhere

AT THE RENO HILTON: Tony Morewood, a finalist in this year's "Star Search" competition, appears in the Just For Laughs Comedy Club through Nov. 13.

Morewood considers his comedy to be "witty, left of center and even a bit expressionistic." Morewood has also appeared on "Comedy on the Road" and MTV's "Half Hour Comedy Hour."

Country comic Gary Mule Deer rides into town starting Nov. 15. He'll perform nightly through Nov. 20.

Show times are Tuesday, Wednesday, Thursday and Sunday at 8:30 p.m. Times for shows on Friday and Saturday are at 8:30 p.m. and 10:30 p.m. Tickets are $9.95 plus tax except Saturday when they are $12.95 plus tax.

Details: 789-2285.

After Steel Breeze, it's the nostalgic soul sounds of Sonny Turner in the Cabaret Lounge beginning Nov. 15 and ending Nov. 27.

AT THE ELDORADO: Rob Hanna's salute to Rod Stewart plays nightly through Nov. 13. Flip Orley, a comic hypnotist, appears in the Cabaret from Nov. 15 through Nov. 27.

For ticket prices or details call: 786-5700.

AT HARRAH'S LAKE TAHOE: The dynamic duo, Gary and Sandy, take the Casino Center Stage through Nov. 13. The pair provide an entertaining mix of humor and music.

The powerful vocals of Jackie Landrum and Inside Out fill the stage on Nov. 12 through Nov. 14. Sweet Louie and the Checkmates, an eight-piece horn band from Las Vegas, perform from Nov. 15 through Nov. 27.

AT THE PEPPERMILL: Cameron, Power House and Zella Lehr appear in the lounge through Nov. 13.

Starting Nov. 14, it's rockers Madison Avenue and impressionist David Proud along with Double Edge.

AT HARVEY'S: Art Vargas & Two Sweet, along with Madison Avenue, play the Emerald Party Lounge through Nov. 13.

Then it's Reta & the Wizz Kidz starting Nov. 14 and Glenn Williams beginning Nov. 15. Williams plays a mix of '50s and '60s do-wop, rhythm and blues, nostalgia and country music.

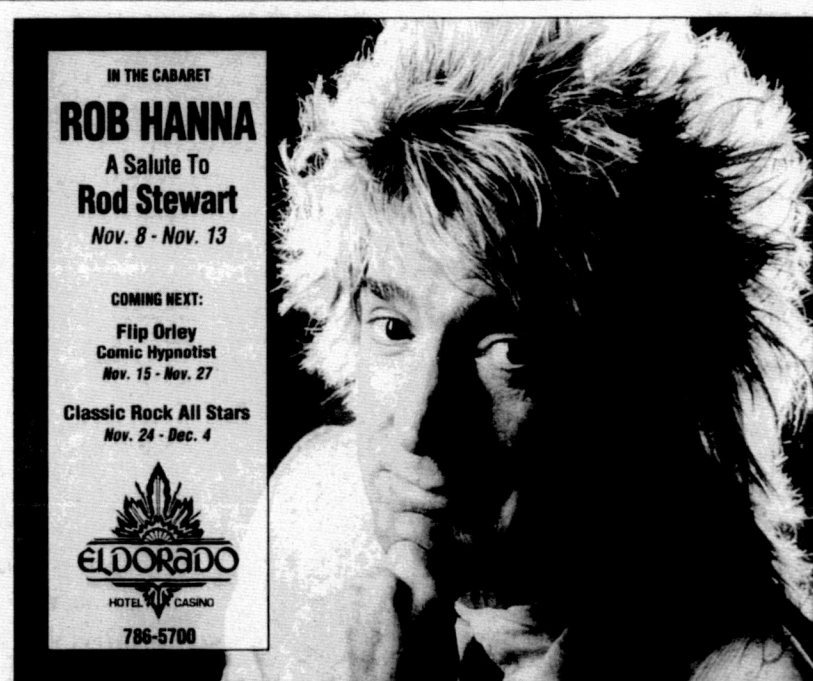

Bump & Grind

HILL TOP PRODUCTIONS
PRESENTS

THE SONS OF CHAMPLIN

BUMP AND GRIND

FRIDAY 13
FEBRUARY
8:00 P.M.
$5.00 ADVANCE
$5.50 DOOR

AT THE
VETERANS HALL
IN
TRUCKEE

ADVANCE TICKETS
truckee: Earthsongs
tahoe city: Stereoscope
reno: Mirabellis
kings beach: 11-7 WHATEVER SHOP

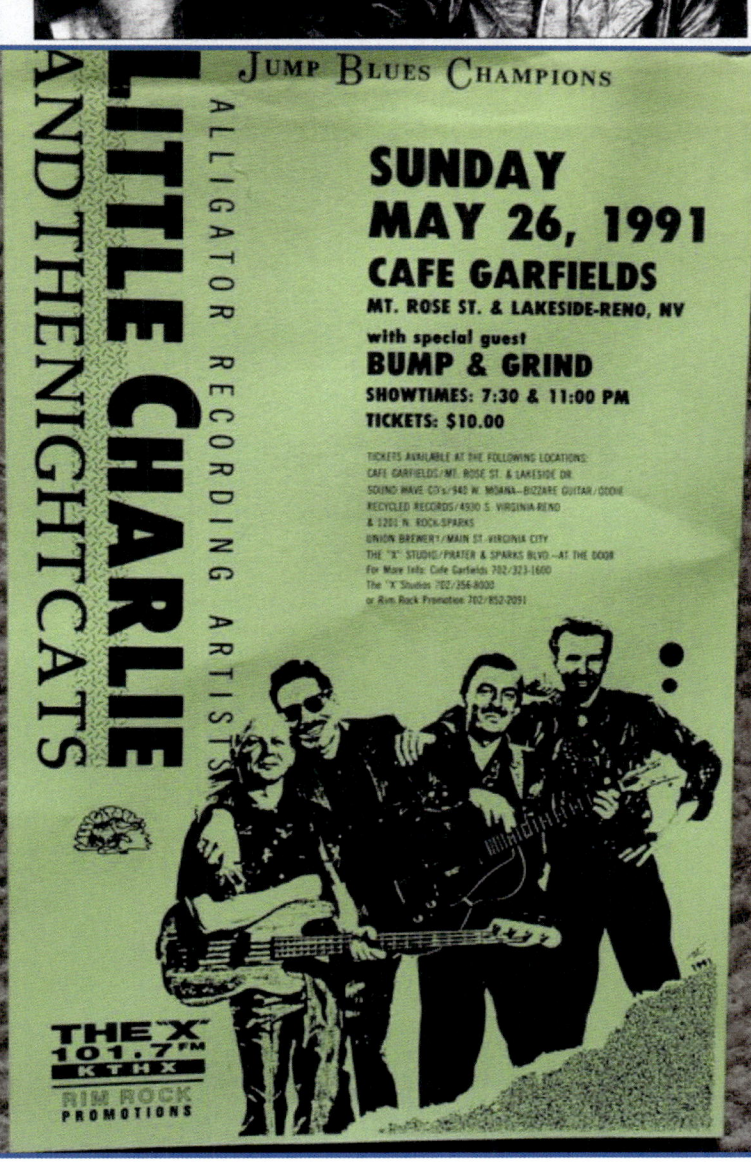

JUMP BLUES CHAMPIONS

ALLIGATOR RECORDING ARTISTS

LITTLE CHARLIE AND THE NIGHTCATS

SUNDAY
MAY 26, 1991
CAFE GARFIELDS
MT. ROSE ST. & LAKESIDE-RENO, NV
with special guest
BUMP & GRIND
SHOWTIMES: 7:30 & 11:00 PM
TICKETS: $10.00

TICKETS AVAILABLE AT THE FOLLOWING LOCATIONS:
CAFE GARFIELDS/MT. ROSE ST. & LAKESIDE DR.
SOUND WAVE CD's/940 W. MOANA - BIZZARE GUITAR/ODDIE
RECYCLED RECORDS/4930 S. VIRGINIA-RENO
& 1201 N. ROCK-SPARKS
UNION BREWERY/MAIN ST. VIRGINIA CITY
THE "X" STUDIO/PRATER & SPARKS BLVD - AT THE DOOR
For More Info: Cafe Garfields 702/323-1600
The "X" Studios 702/356-8000
or Rim Rock Promotion 702/852-2091

THE X
101.7 FM
KTHX
RIM ROCK
PROMOTIONS

PABLO CRUISE

WITH BUMP & GRIND

Thanksgiving Holiday Dance & Show

Fri & Sat November 26 & 27
9pm - 2am
(Doors open at 8:00)

at SDF   DBSU
Squaw Valley
FOOD & SPIRITS

Tickets: $5.00 in advance $6.00 at the door

79

"The New Breed" was a Sacramento band that had a hit single called "Green Eyed Woman" that got airplay on Reno station KCBN in 1965. They played Reno on occasion at the State Building and The Door. Bassist Timothy B. Schmit went on to join "Poco" and, eventually joined the "Eagles", where he is today.

THE NEW BREED

The Sables

1966

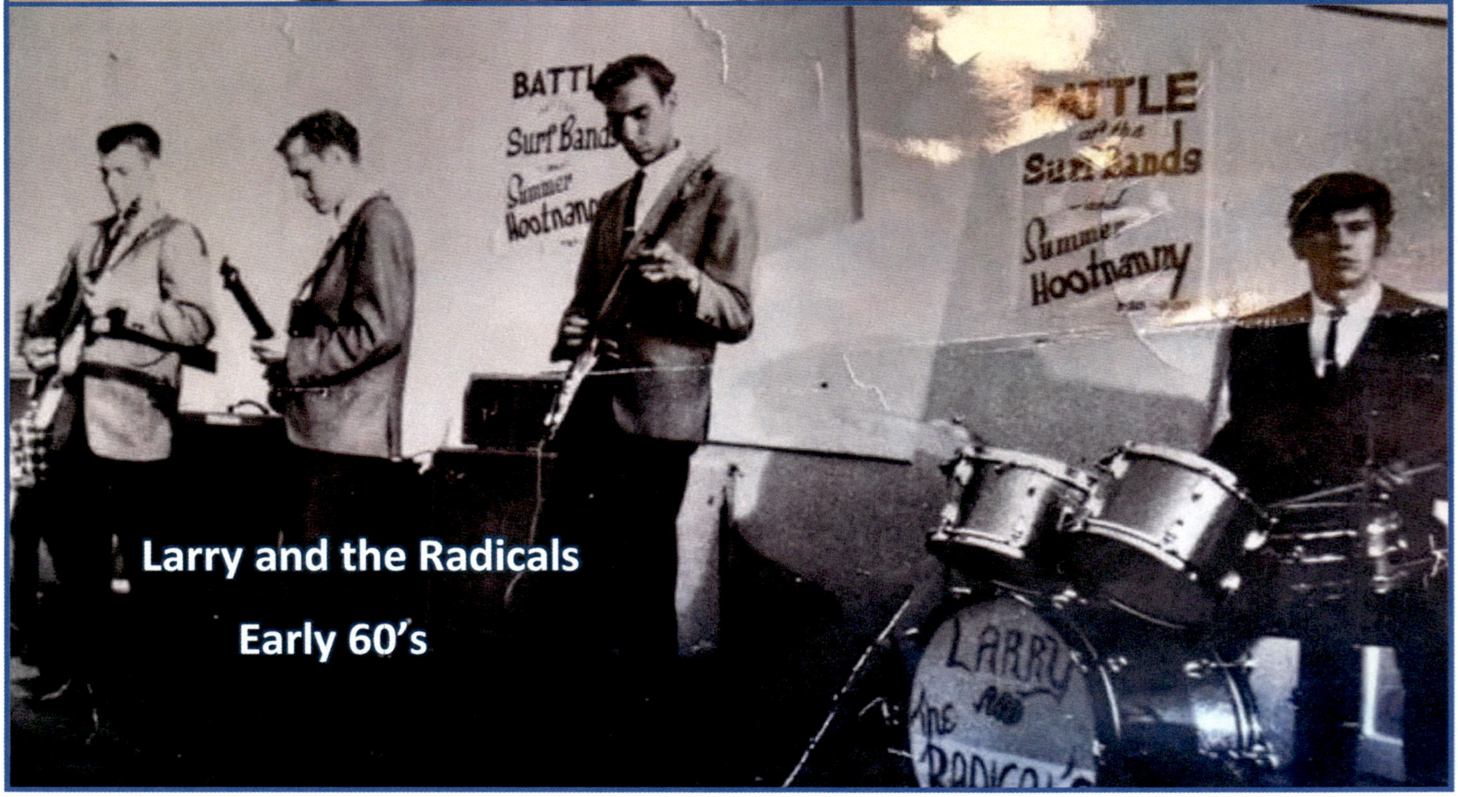

Larry and the Radicals

Early 60's

80

Silent Partner

the **LOOK**

Reno, Nevada

Craig Salioi/Gazette-Journal

ROCK OPERA: Among the performers who will appear in the rock opera "Morrison Mania: An American Festival" are, front row from left, Scott Hazelwood as Ray Manzarek and Raven Ladd as Jim Morrison; back row from left, Michele Lundeen as Janis Joplin; Dana Gutenberger as Grace Slick, Ray Sanchez as Elvis Presley, Tracy Ashton as Marilyn Monroe and Mike Dues as John Belushi. The show starts at 7 p.m. at Reno's Pioneer Theater.

Heaven rocks in Reno show

By Joe De Chick/Gazette-Journal

It was like a scene from rock 'n' roll heaven.

Jim Morrison curled up to the microphone with Janis Joplin while Elvis Presley threw his hair back and chuckled.

Add a leggy, cherry-lipped Marilyn Monroe and a rollicking Mozart, and you've got some of the cast of "Morrison Mania: An American Festival," a rock opera to be performed Saturday at 7 p.m at Reno's Pioneer Theater.

Tickets for the show — which features all local talent and is produced by Paradise Productions of Reno — are $10 in advance and $11 at the door, and can be purchased at the Ticket Station and Budget Tapes & Records.

Local musicians Scott Hazelwood and Raven Ladd wrote the script of the four-act, 3½-half hour show

"This is a tribute to the music of the late Jim Morrison (and his rock group the Doors), his contemporaries and his philosophies," said Hazelwood, a classically trained pianist who will play

among others — Mozart and Scott Joplin.

"The audience will be taken through the life and times of rock 'n' roll and legendary personalities of the past

"A whole show of just Morrison tends to go dry after a while. We want to incorporate other characters and dimensions through Morrison."

Ladd and Hazelwood met in a parking lot two years ago. Between them they've spent more than four years

See ROCK, page 40

Dana Cowen (Gutenberger)

The Look

Zeitgeist

Dave Clark

Over a span of nearly 40 years, Dave played bass with some of the most talented groups ever to appear in the Reno-Lake Tahoe area.

Babe Pace with Dave on bass

Madison Ave.

Dave with "Stage Door Johnny" at Paul Revere's "Kicks" 1990

Hacienda Del Sol, Reno— 1989

TEASER

Dave Clark

This is a Ship

Ship of Fools

"Ship of Fools" was a rock band based out of Spokane, Washington.

It featured longtime Reno rockers Rob Hanna and Ric Yancey.

They toured the West extensively in the mid-70's.

These are the **Fools**

Ship of Fools

In community service or in watering holes, Chris Talbot keeps the music, the fun — and the challenges — flowing

ON STAGE: Chris Talbot at Cantina Los Tres Hombres.

Joe Gosen/Gazette-Journal

Court Jester of Reno

David Parker/Gazette-Journal

CHRIS TALBOT: The veteran Reno performer, right, hosts open-mike night on Thursdays at Cantina Los Tres Hombres.

AVALANCHE

AVALANCHE

Ted Nugent at the Coliseum — a review

By MARK CRAWFORD

With the opening assistance of a more sophisticated musical act, Reno's own A la Mode, Ted Nugent and three sidemen acted Thursday night like Hoover-Dam dynamos for a sellout crowd of about 7,000 in the Centennial Coliseum.

Nugent, self-styled the "Motor City Madman" for his Detroit associations, is anything but Motown. Yet, at his best, he stole devices of soul from black music of the 1960s, pouring some emotion over the denatured hard rock candy Nugent force-feeds his young audiences.

The audience swallowed it all — from the smoke bomb to the more valuable long excursions in simple modes, where Nugent played some equally simple, clean guitar lines.

His lyrics were the opposite of clean. In fact, they had all the grit and sludge of a rag pile under a Motor City grease rack. But again, the Reno crowd scarfed it all up and demanded more.

More in this case included some heavily synthe-sized entr'acte chords sounded very loud for two minutes plus. Again, the modal idea — major and minor thirds fading in and out — a body trip for sure, as much of the sound was no doubt below the human ear's frequency response.

Nugent's own ears, of course, are reputedly cotton-stuffed beneath his enviable locks of dishwater blond. Reputedly, he's down to 15 percent hearing efficiency in the left ear. But, in the slow "Strangle Hold" with drummed double time, for example, he showed superior musical sensibilities to his heavy-metal Reno concert predecessor Van Halen. And his theater, though hardly impeccable, at least was interestingly peccable.

He handled the hair, the bare chest (thumped with a microphone in a heart-breaking introduction to an unprintable heart-aching introduction of a song about poontang), and the coontail hanging down his backside with a good sense of drama — the kind which demands dramamine.

But the audience, rather than breaking the downstage barricade and wasting time throwing up — again an improvement on the Van Halen response, which was visceral more than vocal.

Concert producer Michael Schivo need hardly have delivered his now-classic "Everybody Take Two Steps Back" speech. The barricade held, and so did Nugent's control.

Opening act A la Mode, in its present form for about six months, was if anything in finer form musically. The locals (reportedly Steve Hobson, guitar; Steve Hatley, keyboards; Jerry Weems, bass and lead vocals; Steve Self, drums) showed much subtler manipulation of their material, at least surviving a half-dozen numbers without being shouted down by "We want Ted."

Building from solid foundations in rock, with a sprinkling of Latin innuendo, the group leaned on Weems' strong vocal presence. Highlighting it all was Self, whose trap-set backbeat hit the proper note between sophistication and a slap in the face.

His drum solo challenged even Rob Hanna's impressive Rod Stewart impression on "Do You Think I'm Sexy?" and Nugent himself for spotlight honors, in all musical honesty.

PHARAOH'S
364 WATER ST. GASTOWN B.C.

A' LA MODE

FEB. 26 ⇆ MAR. 10

THE
MOTHERLODE
PRESENTS
A' LA MODE

Back by popular demand
JULY 24–29

HWY. 50 & KAHLE DR.
LAKE TAHOE, NEV.

VALENTINO
A LA MODE
AUGUST 24, 25, 26
FRI, SAT, and SUN
SHIRE ROAD PUB
··one block east of winding way & sunrise in fair oaks··

SHEPHERD.   ©73 SHEPHERD STUDIOS

A' La Mode—1979

Steve Self, Jerry Weems, Steve Hobson, Steve Hatley

Cheryl Cotten: A Brief History

Cheryl Cotten, arguably Reno's most well-known female fiddle player, got her start touring with Sammie Smith ("Help Me Make It Through the Night") in 1975. During college at Texas Tech University, Cheryl won fiddle contests, sat in with The Texas Playboys, Merle Haggard, and Asleep at the Wheel. She turned down a job offer from Merle, choosing instead to finish earning her degree in violin performance. In 1979 and 1980 Cheryl performed with Willow Springs, a band headed up by Stan Lark, original member of The Fireballs (#1 hit in 1963 "Sugar Shack") and opened shows for Ferlin Husky, Hank Thompson, Jerry Wallace, and The Hagar Twins.

In 1980 Cheryl put together The Cheryl Cotten Band, with Joseph DeRosa on keys and vocals, Ron Rummage on bass, trumpet and vocals, and Jammey Kidd on drums. Although musicians came and went, Joseph stayed with Cheryl for the rest of their road days. Cheryl's band opened for or shared the stage with Sonny Turner, Donna Fargo, Charlie Pride, Susan Raye, and BJ Thomas, and played venues in the US and Canada. The band frequented showrooms in Reno, including Fitzgerald's, Harrah's, Harald's Club, John Asquaga's Nugget, and Las Vegas at the Union Plaza and Hilton. Cheryl earned a RAMA award (Reno Area Music) in 1985, and in 1988 appeared on the cover of Fun & Gaming, the leading Reno entertainment magazine.

Cheryl also played trumpet, as she covered music by Chicago and Blood, Sweat & Tears in her shows, along with other horns in the band.

It was around 1984 when Cheryl was featured in a band, "Command Performance." They were performing at the Playboy Club in Omaha, Nebraska. For the show opener the band would begin a song with Cheryl off stage. She would suddenly appear in the back of the room playing her wireless violin as the spot light followed her up to the stage. But at this particular gig, her heel caught the hem of her dress as she stepped up to the stage, pulling her dress far enough down to earn her Bunny status. Pro that she was, she continued playing, her back to the audience, holding her violin close, in an attempt to maintain her dignity. Despite her efforts, the drummer, for a moment, had the best seat in the house.

It was in Laughlin, Nevada, where a huge storm flooded the whole town. Cheryl's band was set up at the newly built Edgewater Casino, but they were afraid to enter the stage and fire up the sound system, because water was streaming down from the light sockets, right on to the stage. An attempt was made to vacuum the water from the carpet, and management "encouraged" the band to perform, which they did, for fear of losing the gig. Their footsteps made squishing sounds as they walked across the stage. There was a puddle of water on the Yamaha Electric Grand. When they turned on the gear, the 16-channel mixer fried. Luckily, they had a small spare.

Cheryl was known for her unique rendition of "The Devil Went Down to Georgia," for which she consistently received standing O's, and in 2018 was invited to perform it with the Reno Wind Symphony. In 1989 Cheryl and husband Joseph DeRosa wrote and produced a Christmas song, "Little Ones Love Christmas," which enjoyed regular rotation on five major Reno radio stations that year.

During the 90s Cheryl and Joseph continued gigging as a duo, and produced jingles for Reno businesses including The Peppermill and Port of Subs. They performed for Artown, conventions, and with local bands, as they opened for major artists such as Blood, Sweat & Tears, Starship, Ambrosia, and Johnny Rivers. Throughout 2020 and 2021 Cheryl and Joseph performed with Papa Clutch & the Shifters, led by Dave McDowell, after which Cheryl began her semi-retirement doing gigs and recordings with Joseph, teaching, and playing trumpet in the Reno Wind Symphony.

1982

When Cheryl Cotten fiddles, people listen

Can a trained concert violinist find happiness as a Top Forty fiddler? Folks who spend an evening with the Cheryl Cotten Band at Fitzgerald's Cabaret Lounge will have little doubt.

Quiet and soft-spoken, an occasional hint of country graces her speech. "I speak through my music" she says, and indeed, as she takes the stage her energy is infectious as she plays and sings with charm and enthusiasm. No one could perform with such exuberance as Ms. Cotten and not like their work.

Born in Germany and raised in the south, Cheryl started playing the violin at the age of thirteen and continued her studies at Texas Tech University with the goal of becoming a concert violinist.

Why the switch? "In a symphony you are only one of the crowd - no one hears or cares if you make a mistake," explains Cheryl. "As a stage performer, I'm an individual - I can be myself, and create the atmosphere I want."

Renoites first noticed Cheryl while she was working with the locally popular Willow Springs band, and her country fiddling was said by many to be the drawing attraction for that group.

She has also played with such country greats as Tex Williams, Jimmy Rogers, the Haggar Bros., Ferlin Husky and the country-rock group Asleep At The Wheel. Last spring she received great reviews as she shared the marquee with Montana at John Ascuaga's Nugget in Sparks.

Those in the audience who are familiar with her work are in for a surprise with Cheryl's new show. The hot fiddling continues, but the music has changed to soft rock, featuring hits by Chicago, Steely Dan, The Charlie Daniels Band and some of The Cheryl Cotten Band's own tunes.

CHERYL COTTEN BAND

"We're very excited about the new direction the band is taking. I use the violin in virtually every piece we do. There are no other pop/rock performers featuring this instrument that I know of - the versatility of the fiddle (violin) has yet to be explored in rock music."

In fact, the instrument Cheryl uses is a "viola," (a slightly larger violin, for those not musically educated) which she has modified by adding an extra string.

Not only is Cheryl an excellent violinist, she plays a mean trumpet, often performing in duet with bassist Ron Rummage. Ron, by the way, astounds the audience by performing simultaneously on the trumpet and the bass guitar. They are joined on stage by trained percussionist Jammey Kidd, and Joseph DeRosa on keyboard.

The Cheryl Cotten Band will keep things moving nightly through Feb. 27 in Fitzgerald's Cabaret Lounge.

1985

Cheryl Cotten

FUN & GAMING

Cheryl Cotten

Peppermill Hotel Casino

1988

C
R
Y
S
T
A
L

I
M
A
G
E

Foolish Behaviour

Foolish Behaviour

Jim Burgett Presents — Live in Lake Tahoe

Aum.. Wayne Ceballos
Beautiful Day
Birmingham Sunday
Brother Rock
Buddy Miles Express
Cascades
Chambers Brothers
Chapman Brothers
Charlie Mussel White
Chuck Berry
Cold Blood
Country Weather
Electric Prunes
Elvin Bishop
Family Tree
Flamin Grooves
Grateful Dead
Guess Who
Justice Five
John Lee Hooker
Kenny O Dell
Muddy Waters
Neighborhood Childr'n
Phoebe Snow
Ratz
Sanpaku
Santana
Sir Douglas Quintet
Sons of Chaplin
Spinning Wheel with Jim Burgett
Steve Miller
Steppenwolf
Stoneground (became Pablo Cruise)
Svelts (became Fanny)
Taj Mahal
Them
Tower of Power
Velvet Chain
Wally Cox (soul singer)
Wayne Cochran (CC Riders)
Weather Macher
Whalers (with Johnny Greek)
Young Bloods... Get Together Right Now

Jim Burgett and Mike Mantor Party on!

Jim Burgett performed at and promoted countless dances and concerts at South Lake Tahoe in the 60's and 70's.

A true legend in the Reno/Tahoe history of rock 'n' roll!

Jim Burgett
American Legion Hall

FOR DEMONSTRATION
USE ONLY
NOT FOR SALE

15915

COLUMBIA

333 RPM

3-41962
2"Lp" 53096

THE LIVING DEAD
- W. Weidter -

JIM BURGETT
with Don Ralke and
his Orchestra

"COLUMBIA". MARCAS REG.
PRINTED IN U.S.A.

The Saddle Tramps
First incarnation—1998

101

THE SADDLE TRAMPS

WHISKEY DICK

PARENTAL ADVISORY EXPLICIT LYRICS

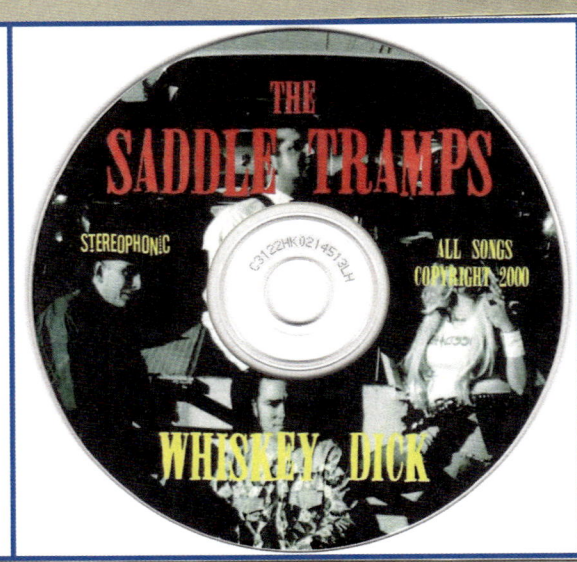

1. MAMMA WAS A FLAGGER**
(S. Roller, R. Harvey R. Hanna)

2. WAITIN' ON A WAITRESS ***
(J. Von Nolde, S. Roller, M. Mantor)

3. AFTER A SIXER**
(J. Von Nolde, S. ROller)

4. (YOU PUT THE % #^! IN COUNTRY**
(J. Von Nolde, S. Roller)

5. THAT AIN'T RIGHT**
(J Von Nolde, S. Roller)

6. CONSUELA***
(S. Roller, J. Von Nolde)

7. RING OF FIRE*
(J. Carter, M. Kilgore)

* Produced By Steven Swinford

** Produced By Steven Swinford And the SaddleTramps

*** Produced By Steven Swinford And Phil Cristian
And The SaddleTramps

PRODUCED BY THE SADDLE TRAMPS
Recorded by Steven Swinford And Phil Cristian

THE SADDLE TRAMPS

WHISKEY DICK

1. Shakin' In My Boots
2. Sweatin'
3. Home Sweet Homo
4. New Diet
5. Film At Eleven
6. Truck Drivin' Lover
7. Cindy Brady (Have My Baby)
8. Liquored Up & Feelin' Down
9. Bye Bi Baby
10. El Boracho
11. College
12. Spoiled Rich Kid
13. The Mullet Song
14. Piggy Sue
15. White Trash Intro
16. White Trash Chicks On Speed
*17. Rebel Yell (1st Take)
*18. Vag For Men

Produced by Steve Swinford & The Saddle Tramps except track 18
Track 18 produced & engineered by Nick Danger

WWW.THESADDLETRAMPS.COM

041472081677

THE SUTRO BAND

The Sutro Band has a legendary reputation
in Northern Nevada and California. Having
entertained in the area for over 12 years
the band was voted BEST ROCK GROUP in the
RENO AREA MUSIC AWARDS (RAMA) in 1984.
Offering a variety of musical entertainment
from the classic Motown hits to Rhythm and
Blues to contemporary Top 40, the Sutro
Band is for all occasions.

FRED MYER - DRUMS: Formerly with recording artists Dave Mason and Commander Cody.
Fred is a dynamic, powerful drummer playing Rock, Funk, Reggae or Jazz.
Fred has played professionally for fifteen years and originates from the
San Francisco area.

SCOTT MYER - LEAD & RHYTHM GUITAR, LEAD & BACK-UP VOCALS: Formerly with recording
artist Commander Cody. Scott is a song writer as well as performer
with deep roots in Rhythm and Blues. Together with his twin brother,
Fred, he has represented the Sutro Band for over seven years.

DANNY HULL - ALTO & TENOR SAX, LEAD & BACK-UP VOCALS: Formerly with recording
artists "Cold Blood". A local favorite, Danny is known for his
"incredible" sax solos. Danny is a published song writer and has
played with Sutro for six years.

JERRY WEEMS - BASS GUITAR, LEAD GUITAR, LEAD & BACK-UP VOCALS: A very versatile
musician, Jerry sings and plays the classics as well as contemporary
tunes with inspiring dexterity. Formerly he played with recording
artist Edgar Winter. Originating from Central California Jerry has
been a Sutro member for four years.

RICH LEWIS - TROMBONE, LEAD & BACK-UP VOCALS, PERCUSSION: Formerly with Columbia
recording artists "Little John". Also from the San Francisco area
Rich attended Cabrillo College in Santa Cruz majoring in music.
Currently performing as a guest artist at Lake Tahoe clubs and
casinos, Rich has been a Sutro regular for two years.

JACKIE LARR - LEAD & BACK-UP VOCALS: A professional singer for over fifteen
years, Jackie is Sutro's newest member. After five years on the
Nevada circuit performing in casinos, clubs and commercials, she
joined Sutro in January of 1986. Another versatile artist, Jackie sings
Rhythm & Blues, Rock, and easy-listening Top 40.

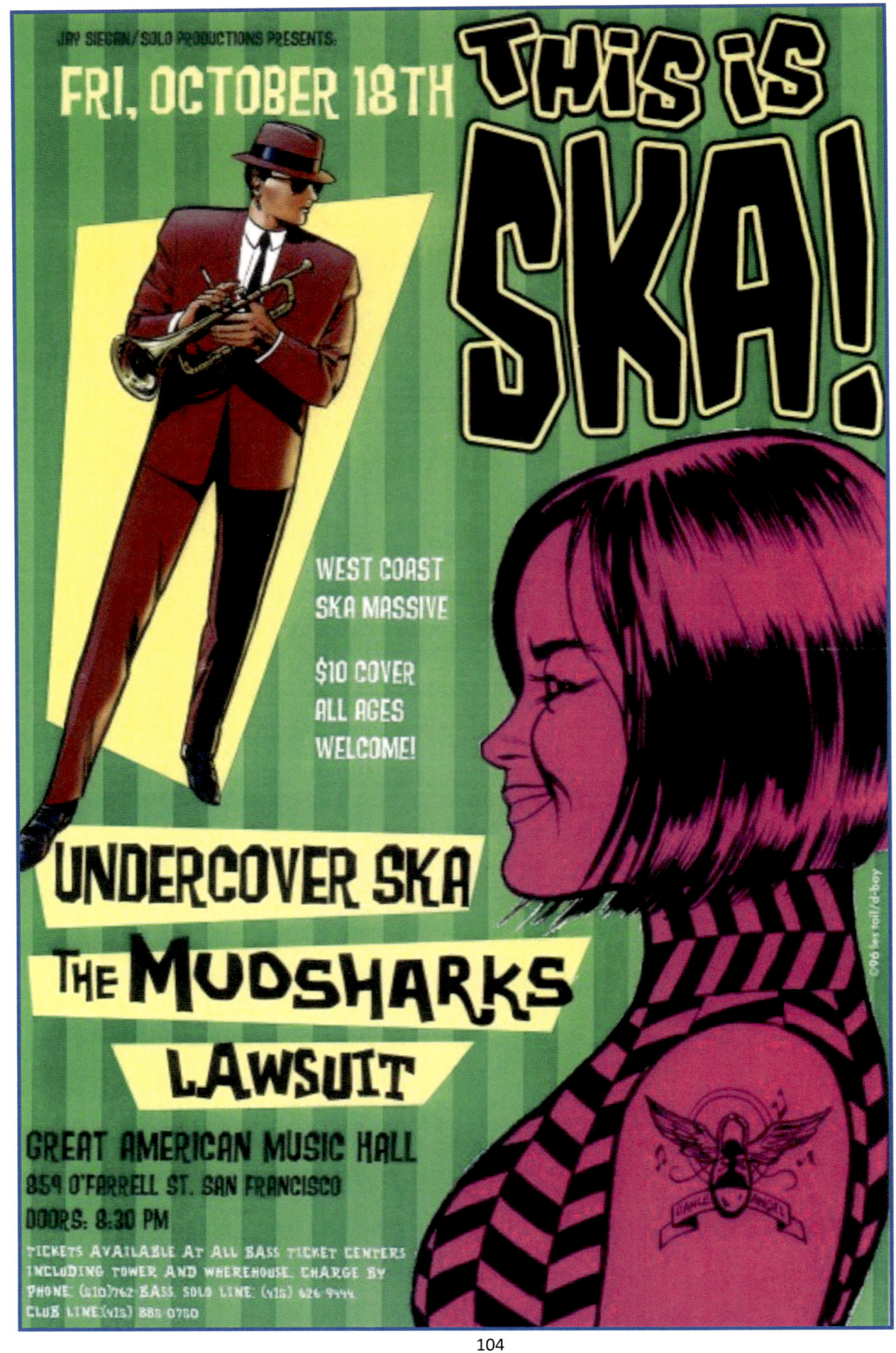

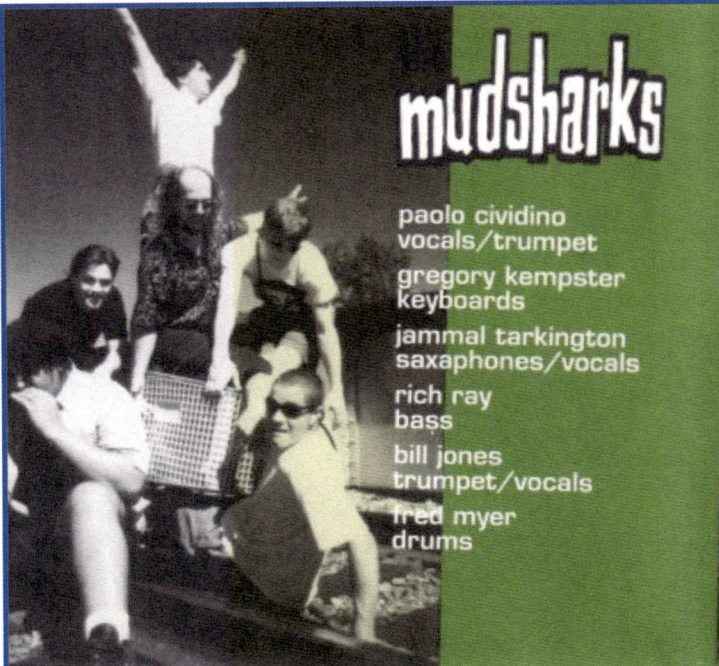

mudsharks

paolo cividino
vocals/trumpet

gregory kempster
keyboards

jammal tarkington
saxaphones/vocals

rich ray
bass

bill jones
trumpet/vocals

fred myer
drums

crackin' porcelain

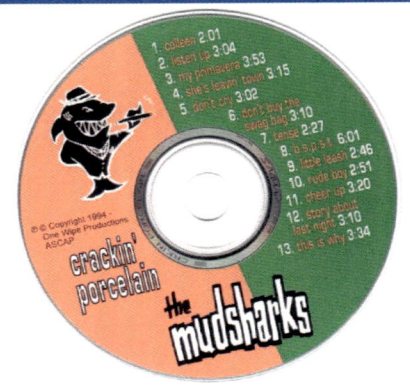

The music rolls on this mid-October weekend, starting with **The Refreshments** from Phoenix, Ariz.

I had the pleasure of seeing this band perform last March in Austin, Tex. and I asked them right then and there to bring their brand of high-energy rock 'n' roll to Lake Tahoe!

Very witty lyrics, crisp guitar and driving rhythm section make the Refreshments the ticket this Friday, Oct. 20 at Humpty's!

Reno's own ska stars **The Mudsharks** are coming off a national tour opening for the Selectors.

They are coming home to Tahoe to play a headlining performance on Saturday, Oct.

Brent Dana

21 at Humpty's. Tix are only $5 for the Sharks!

The **Grey Boy Allstars** are an extremely talented young band! They have taken years of jazz experience and combined elements of funk, calypso and rock 'n' roll into a very groovy fusion that is nearly impossible to hold still to!

It's going to be a celebration of music when the Allstars take the stage Sunday, Oct. 22 at Humpty's Lake Tahoe. Tix are $5 for this must-see show!

Ready or not Halloween cometh, with the holiday season and winter close behind. Enjoy!

Peace! ♦

Brent Dana is a local music promoter.

THE MUDSHARKS
OCT. 21 AT HUMPTY'S.

106

Paolo Cividino • Vocals, trumpet
Matthew Francis • Guitar
Greg Kempster • Keyboards
Fred Myer • Drums
Rich Ray • Bass
Jammal Tarkington • Saxes, vocals
Bill Jones • Trumpet, flugelhorn, vocals

the mudsharks

FOR BOOKINGS CALL:

Rich Ray
1.800. 626.8901
702. 786.4500
Fred Myer
702. 747.9014

Milestone—1978

2nd Coming—1973

**Bobby Dee and Company
1991**

JUDY LYNN

SILVER STRAINS: Easy Street performs strong instrumentals and tight harmonies at the Silver Club Hotel Casino on Victorian Square in Sparks. This group fills the Gazebo lounge with rock, pop and country. Show times: 358-4771

On the Cover . . . .

Elijah—1973

Skid Kids—1985

Ethyl Myrtz—1996

Wilder Street

The Candymen—1965
At The Caboose in Sparks

The Lost & Found
Carson City Civic Auditorium—1966

Chuck Ruff 1951—2011

Fat Chance—Mid 80's

Fat Chance—Mid 80's

116

Michael Furlong – "The Last Man Standing"

I grew up in a family with two brothers and two sisters, a lot of aunts, uncles, grandparents and cousins...none of whom played musical instruments. My parents, Bill and Eve, loved music and I heard The Platters, Bing Crosby, Frank Sinatra, Dean Martin, Nat King Cole, Sammy Davis Jr., and even Al Jolson and Spike Jones. I appreciated their music but never really subscribed to it myself. The one that stood out to me was Dean Martin. What a class act!

My love of music kicked in when I began listening to The Beach Boys, The Beatles, The Rolling Stones, The Kinks, The Yardbirds, and The Byrds. A relative left an acoustic guitar at our house and I started to play around with it. My first challenge was to learn "Dirty Water" by The Standells. I played it with only 5 strings, over and over. I eventually learned how to change strings with the help of Maytan Music in Carson City.

I began to sing along with The Beach Boys and The Beatles which led to my role as lead vocalist in the "Shades of Blue" in 1968. At 13 years of age Jim Johns, Jack Randell, Jim Honyumptewa, Mike Giardano (Joe LaChew's stepbrother), formed that band. We worked hard at it and eventually did our first live performance at the Carson Community Center, opening for Joe's up and coming band, "Birmingham Sunday". I loved playing guitar and practiced relentlessly. My first rig was a Silvertone semi-acoustic guitar with a dual-channel Silvertone amp. Wished I'd kept it! I showed up to a band rehearsal with my new equipment, yet unbeknownst to my band mates. From then on, I was lead vocalist and rhythm guitarist. I also learned to play piano, bass, drums, flute and trombone.

For a short time I played with a sister act called "Something Nasty". We had limited success performing in the Carson City area for teen and local events like the Nevada State Fair. The sisters moved on to day jobs, and the band broke up.

After high school I continued performing while working for the Carson City School District as the Educational TV Director. At 21 I started playing with Ron and Bonnie Ryser, along with my wife Naunie, Tom Evans, and Bill Campbell in a band called "Double Down". After having some success in the Reno area, the prospect of becoming full-time musicians was proposed. We quit our day jobs, and headed out on the road with Headfirst Productions (Mike and Kathie Mantor) as our booking agency. We eventually went our separate ways, but from then on I remained a career musician.

I was offered a guitar/singer position with a band called "LG Soundcheck" with Lener Gousetis, Brent Harpham and Richard Ray playing the Reno venues.

Disco music was becoming wildly popular. The LGS band renamed ourselves "Satchmo". Lener, Brent, Terry Petersen on bass and I, along with my wife Naunie, played some disco, but mostly funk music. We were living and performing on the Old Sacramento circuit, as well as in Sacramento and Reno venues.

Lener decided on a daytime career, so along with Terry's influence I began a journey into jazz fusion and progressive rock. It was a great experience learning to play some very complex guitar styles.

That led me to join Jimmy Cicero and Steve Self in a band called "Jazuir". We played mostly off-nights in the Reno area while I was teaching at Bizarre Guitar. While the jazz fusion experience was a great way to sharpen my guitar skills, it wasn't popular enough to support a full-time gig.

SATCHMO

Rob Hanna asked if I would join his band "Decker", doing his "Salute to Rod Stewart". We took it to Hawaii in May of 1980.

The Decker/Hawaii gig was to be for 6 weeks but wound up lasting a year. We played military bases and Waikiki nightclubs. While there, I asked to guest on guitar for the Hawaiian rock band "Teazer" on the album they were recording. It was then I met Rick Keefer, the owner and producer of Sea-West Recording Studios. Rick indicated that he would be interested in producing me if I ever returned to Hawaii. I joined "Teazer" briefly, opening concerts for "The Police" and "Cheap Trick".

"Decker" went through some changes with Steve Hobson and John Andreoni joining and we departed to British Columbia to do 6 weeks throughout the province. While there I learned that John Waite had quit "The Babys" and they were looking for a singer. Through some connections, I got an audition. A week before I was to fly to L.A. for the audition, Jonathan Cain quit the band to join "Journey", and that avenue was gone as "The Babys" disbanded.

Back in Reno I was approached by Steve Clausman from Sacramento, to manage our band while offering up some players from the band "Ian Shelter". That was short-lived due to misguided management, though he did manage a success with the band "Tesla".

So, I decided to put another band together and go back to Hawaii to write and record an album. I had secured a performing venue to provide an income there and spoke with Rick at Sea-West who agreed that we'd make a record. The lineup was Terry Petersen, Wayne Brown and Steve Self. Off we went for several years performing venues all over Oahu while writing and recording our album.

Eventually, Steve and Wayne returned to the mainland, and were replaced by Boris Tavcar on drums, and Rich Haines on keyboards. Shortly thereafter Chuck Ruff took over as drummer and our band was called "Boxer". That lineup was very successful, traveling to Guam on a dozen occasions, as well as Oaska, Japan, with Jerry Kratzmeyer now on guitar.

I decided to go back to the mainland to seek out a record deal. After pounding the pavement to death in L.A., I struck interest with Atlantic Records. We were shopping the record as "Michael Furlong" (as a solo artist). With the record titled "Use It Or Lose It", a song from the album. Chuck Ruff and I wrote the song together. The deal was hatched, and I was again faced with assembling a concert-performing lineup. That became Steve Hobson, Chuck Ruff, Daryl Van Dyke, and Doug Caldwell. After another management change I landed interest with Bruce Cohn, who was managing "The Doobie Brothers" and "Night Ranger".

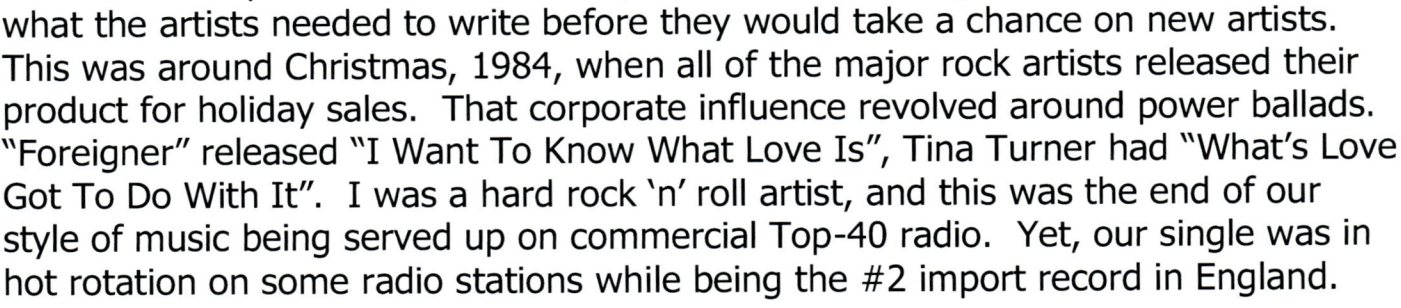

Now, having an Atlantic Records deal with a forthcoming release, and Bruce Cohn Management, I finally appeared to be on my way! We made an MTV video, charted on the Billboard Hot 100 at #72, and performed on "Dick Clark's American Bandstand", "Rock of the 80's" on Showtime, and toured with "Night Ranger" and "Y&T". Playing on this bill at Lawlor Events Center in Reno was quite a thrill!

Sadly, for us, the music industry was becoming a corporate rock enterprise. The record companies were dictating what the artists needed to write before they would take a chance on new artists. This was around Christmas, 1984, when all of the major rock artists released their product for holiday sales. That corporate influence revolved around power ballads. "Foreigner" released "I Want To Know What Love Is", Tina Turner had "What's Love Got To Do With It". I was a hard rock 'n' roll artist, and this was the end of our style of music being served up on commercial Top-40 radio. Yet, our single was in hot rotation on some radio stations while being the #2 import record in England.

I was approached about writing a song for the film, "St. Elmo's Fire". John Parr was the other consideration. At the time I was having serious political complications with Atlantic Records President Doug Morris, Bruce Cohn Management, as well as my production company Sea-West. There was animosity between them as to how to proceed with the promotion. Atlantic passed on renewing my option, as well as some other hard rock bands. Every person involved at this point went their separate ways.

It's now 1985. I'm living in Sacramento, having to form yet another group to perform in rock clubs, along with other bands like "Steel Breeze", "Bourgeois Tag", and "City Kid" (who became "Tesla"). It was around this time when the bar scene hit a brick wall due to tough new drunk-driving laws. Attendance numbers declined dramatically, and we went for 6 nights a week to 2 nights a week. It just wasn't worth working that circuit anymore.

I went back to Guam to attempt a solo, computerized project. I picked up sponsors from Hong Kong Bank, Computer Land, and Budweiser. The effort was a success and I learned a lot.

I then went back to Sacramento where I started work on my new album, "Breakaway". I programmed the drum parts on the Landrum machine, played the bass tracks, sang the lead tracks, and most of the background vocals. I considered it to be a demo, and sent it over to my production company, Sea-West Studios. They agreed to fly me to Hawaii to record a master version of that material. But...the demo project was released in Europe without my knowledge. Apparently, Rick had decided to cash out the record for himself by selling the masters to Music For Nations Records. I made money on the residuals, but did not endorse the record because I considered it a demo.

Then I was approached by a Portland band called "Wild Dogs" to write and record an album as lead vocalist. That lineup was Jeff Mark, Dean Castronovo (who went on to join "Journey" as their drummer), and Rick Bartel. The album was going great but the record label, Enigma Records, went bankrupt and the record was dead.

I now considered casinos to be the final frontier for rock 'n' roll. I rejoined "Rob Hanna's Salute to Rod Stewart", touring the United States and Canada. Toward the end of my stay with Rob, casino budgets began to tank and it appeared that Rob would not be doing his show much longer. I decided to go on my own, doing my Tom Petty tribute and Michael Furlong Band at casinos, fairs, and special events. I've been doing that now for 30 years.

In the meantime I met Jerry Corbetta, lead singer of "Sugarloaf", whose hits had included "Green-Eyed Lady" and "Don't Call Us, We'll Call You". He wanted to put "Sugarloaf" back together, so Omar Martinez from Paul Revere's band, and Dennis Noda from "Sam The Sham and the Pharaohs" joined us. That venture culminated with Dennis committing suicide and Jerry passing away from frontal-lobe dementia. The new version of "Green-Eyed Lady" that we recorded featured Dave Clark on bass, and wound up on a classic rock compilation album.

I'm fortunate to have spent my adult life as a musician. What remained were fair dates, festivals, special events, and casino lounge work. I still perform with a lineup that's been with me for 12 years now. I also work in the industry as a concert audio technician in the Reno-Tahoe area.

Michael Furlong's "Petty Theft"
A Tribute to Tom Petty and the Heartbreakers

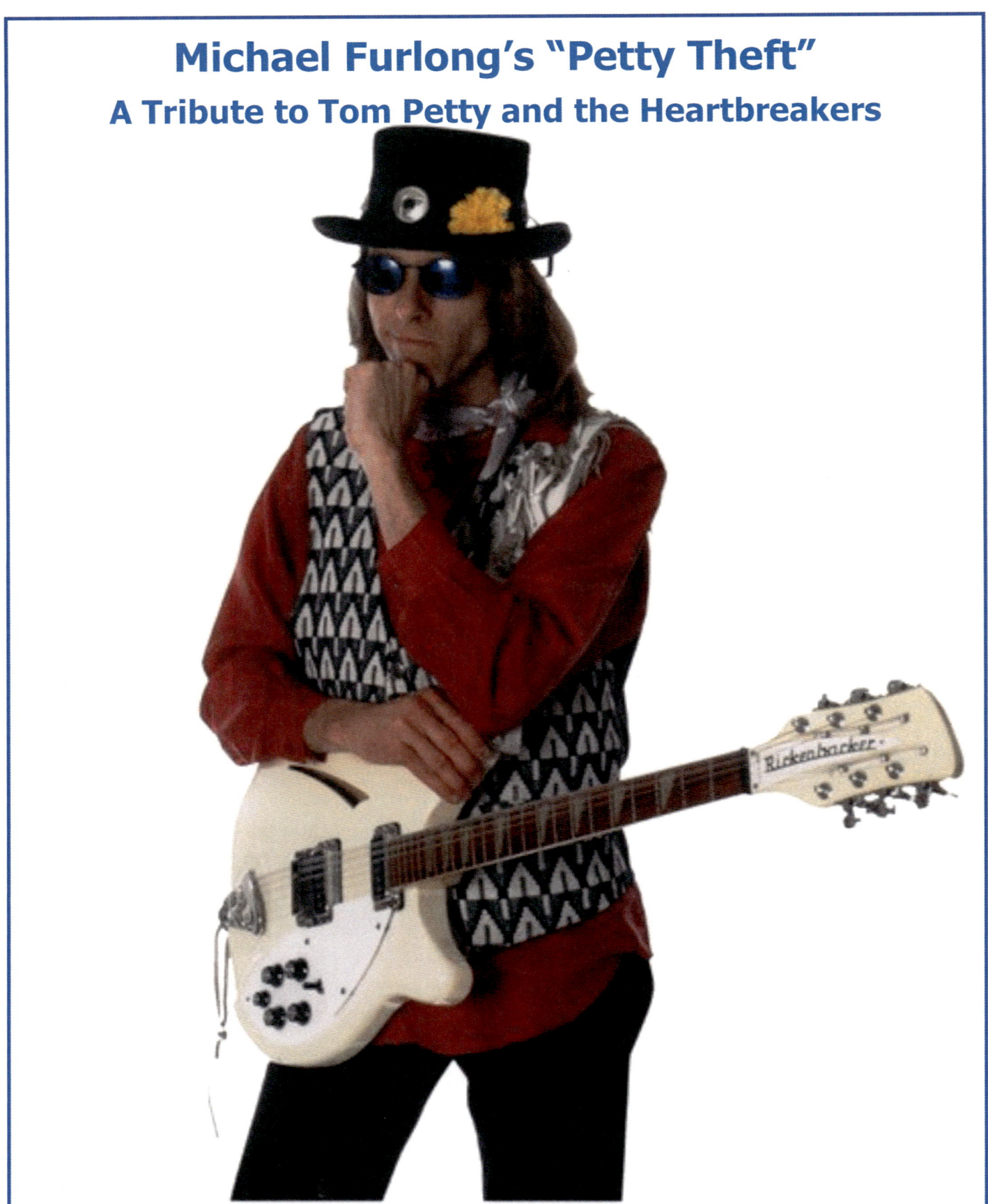

Raised On Radio *"The Tributes"*

Bonnie Raitt

ZZ Top

Rod Stewart

Janis Joplin

Bryan Adams

John Fogerty

Ann Wilson

Huey Lewis

Tom Petty

That's Entertainment 916-853-2777

Steve Hatley (left), Rob Hanna (right), and "Wild Dogs" in the middle-Guam, 1984

Metalscape metal (mĕt′l) n. 1. Any of a class of substances which typically show a peculiar luster, are

scape (skāp), n. (L. scapus shaft arising at the surface of the ground as the bloodroot, tulip, stem, stalk.)

Wild Dogs

The tail-sorry tale began in Portland, Or when **WILD DOGS** recorded their first tracks which proved sufficiently manic to find their way onto Shrapnel Records' U.S. *METAL VOLUME II* and Portland's KGON compilation album. These first tracks proved auspicious enough to result in a deal with Shrapnel Records and the release of their eponymously-titled debut album in March 1983.

The **WILD DOGS** album was racking up glowing praise all over the world, and another track on U.S. *METAL VOLUME III* served to keep the fires burning as the band tore into their second album, *MAN'S BEST FRIEND*. To follow were a series of live shows which were, true to the standards of the band, the most animalistic public performances this side of an ice hockey match.

Now, with the release of *REIGN*

OF TERROR by Enigma Records, these deranged metal meisters will be chasing a lot more cars and mailmen.

Previously, a wolf in sheep's clothing, Michael Furlong adds menacing bite to the album (sounding a bit like Lemmy) and debues as vocalist , replacing Matthew T., a vinyl onslaught of sustained ferocity spearheaded by Jeff Marks' manic guitar and stoked to the boiling point by the furious rhythms of bassist Rick Bartel (replacing Danny Kurthand) and drummer Tom Moller taking his seat after Deen Castronova's departure.

With Furlong, Bartel, Moller and Mark, **WILD DOGS** have taken off in a powerful direction that is unrestrained and total metal.

If you are troubled by traces of sanity, maybe **WILD DOGS** aren't for you. But lovers of danger and

decibels will find *REIGN OF TERROR* the heaviest medicine. Be ready for further announcements. Be on the look-out for strays, with a national tour in the works, **WILD DOGS** may invade your hometown with their rabid metal attack. **DOGS** guitarist Jeff Mark completed a whirlwind promotional tour of Europe where he barked up trees from Madrid to Finland while lead vocalist Michael Furlong spent time sowing his wild oats in Guam. Now **WILD DOGS** are back home preparing a series of live performances in support of their new work and awaiting departure for their 1987 tour.

Release for **WILD DOGS** third L.P. entitled *REIGN OF TERROR* is scheduled for October 3 (Receptor/Greenworld label in Europe and the U.K., ENIGMA in the US). For more information, write to: WILD DOGS FAN CLUB, P.O. Box 42563, San Francisco, CA. 94142.

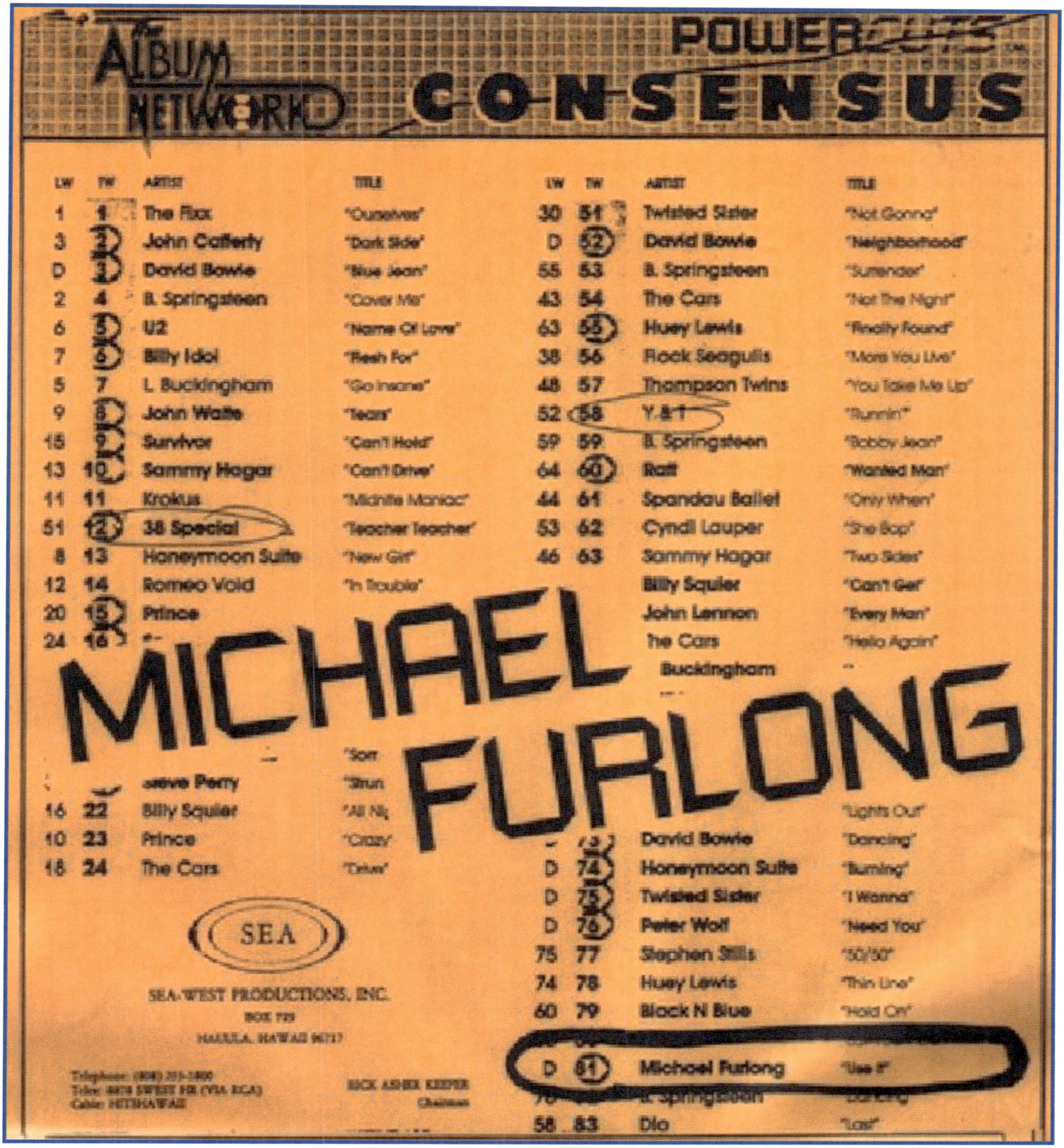

THE ALBUM NETWORK — POWERCUTS CONSENSUS

LW	TW	ARTIST	TITLE	LW	TW	ARTIST	TITLE
1	1	The Fixx	"Ourselves"	30	51	Twisted Sister	"Not Gonna"
3	2	John Cafferty	"Dark Side"	D	52	David Bowie	"Neighborhood"
D	3	David Bowie	"Blue Jean"	55	53	B. Springsteen	"Surrender"
2	4	B. Springsteen	"Cover Me"	43	54	The Cars	"Not The Night"
6	5	U2	"Name Of Love"	63	55	Huey Lewis	"Finally Found"
7	6	Billy Idol	"Flesh For"	38	56	Rock Seagulls	"More You Live"
5	7	L. Buckingham	"Go Insane"	48	57	Thompson Twins	"You Take Me Up"
9	8	John Waite	"Tears"	52	58	Y & T	"Runnin'"
15	9	Survivor	"Can't Hold"	59	59	B. Springsteen	"Bobby Jean"
13	10	Sammy Hagar	"Can't Drive"	64	60	Ratt	"Wanted Man"
11	11	Krokus	"Midnite Maniac"	44	61	Spandau Ballet	"Only When"
51	12	38 Special	"Teacher Teacher"	53	62	Cyndi Lauper	"She Bop"
8	13	Honeymoon Suite	"New Girl"	46	63	Sammy Hagar	"Two Sides"
12	14	Romeo Void	"In Trouble"			Billy Squier	"Can't Get"
20	15	Prince				John Lennon	"Every Man"
24	16					The Cars	"Hello Again"
						Buckingham	
		Steve Perry	"Strun"				
16	22	Billy Squier	"All Nig"				"Lights Out"
10	23	Prince	"Crazy"		73	David Bowie	"Dancing"
18	24	The Cars	"Drive"	D	74	Honeymoon Suite	"Burning"
				D	75	Twisted Sister	"I Wanna"
				D	76	Peter Wolf	"Need You"
				75	77	Stephen Stills	"50/50"
				74	78	Huey Lewis	"Thin Line"
				60	79	Black N Blue	"Hold On"
				D	81	Michael Furlong	"Use It"
						B. Springsteen	"Darling"
				58	83	Dio	"Last"

MICHAEL FURLONG

When Michael's album, "Use It Or Lose It" was released in 1984 it received airplay on many radio stations across the country. The video for the single "Use It Or Lose It" was filmed on locations in Reno and went into regular rotation on MTV.

MICHAEL FURLONG

Shades of Blue—1968

Michael Furlong

Chuck Ruff & Michael Furlong
Guam—1983

SATCHMO

Rusty Butz

Rusty Butz, well known in this area, is appearing at Sunshine Fish and Meat Locker Company at South Shore, Lake Tahoe through July 19th. Tuesday through Sunday, midnight till 4:30 a.m. at Round Hill Village.

Rusty Butz midnighting at Sunshine Fish and Meat Factory, Round Hills

Round Hill Village, at South Lake Tahoe, is resounding from midnight till 4:30 a.m. Tuesday through Sundays to the music of Rusty Butz, playing at the Sunshine Fish and Meat Locker Company.

Rusty Butz is a crowd pleasing group who feature a repertoire of well rehearsed top 40, funk, rock, ballad and original tunes who are well known in the local area.

Naunie Gardner is featured female vocalist and keyboard player who enables the band to play music by popular female artists and provides keyboards to the structure of the band sound. Her mother, a professional opera singer and teacher of vocal and piano technique has schooled her well in that field and added ballet dancing to her repertoire.

Bill Campbell on bass guitar and lead is another former member of Double Down, like Naunie and has a very essential influence on the band's original sound.

Brent Zane on drums and back of vocals, has been playing the drums since the age of nine, and his father is a music professor and professional musician and he has taught an award winning son.

On flute, guitar, piano, lead and back up vocals is Joe LaChew, another member with a professional musician father and mother a professional dancer.

Mike Furlong, on guitar and lead and back-up vocals, has been playing guitar for nine years and has been a vocalist for ten. He is also a songwriter.

Chuck Ruff
Group

Tomorrow's Eyes

Danny Mantor
1950-2020

Justus V—Caboose
1965

The Raiders are coming!
The Raiders are coming!

Paul Revere and the Raiders

Live and in
★ person for ★
one night only

It's a Columbus Day
Rock-N-Roll Dance
Party in honor of
Baby Raider's Birthday.
__Monday October 9__
Tickets on sale now
only $10.00
Doors Open 8 PM
Paul Revere &
The Raiders
8:30PM

Followed by
Stage Door
Johnny til 3 A.M.

Free Valet Parking

Paul Revere's
KICKS
786-7500
140 N. Center St. • Downtown

Bill, It's A
PARTY EVERY NIGHT!
...and now we're
Open Days, too!

Relax Paul

SUN & MON 8PM-4AM
TUES-THURS 11AM-4AM
FRI & SAT 11AM-5AM

BILL MEDLEY and PAUL REVERE

Sunday: Massive Beach Party!!!
Monday: 50¢ Draft Beer & $1⁰⁰ Well Drinks • Stage Door Johnny, Live Music till 3:30 a.m.
Tuesday: Stage Door Johnny Returns! till 3:30 a.m.
Wednesday: Live Music by B.B. & the Boomers till 3:30 a.m. • Ladies' Night, free flower & glass of champasgne
Thursday: "Over 30" Thursday, Show ID... Get in Free
Fri. & Sat.: Bop til you drop.

Paul Revere's
KICKS
786-7500
140 N. Center St. • Downtown

PAUL REVERE
& THE
RAIDERS

P.O. Box 19254
Oakland, CA 94619

Pam Moreno
Fan Club Director

PAUL REVERE EXPRESS
GOLD CARD

VALID THRU
6·89

MEMBER SINCE
1776

KICKS   "NEVER LEAVE HOME WITHOUT ME"   RENO

RENO • KICKS

Rain—A Tribute to the Beatles

It isn't raining rain — it's raining Beatles

Rain: A Tribute to the Beatles re-creates the music and mystique of the famed group that captivated and influenced the music and mood of an entire generation. Oct. 29 through Nov. 10, Rain will bring the legendary look and sound of the Beatles to Sammy's Showroom at Harrah's Reno.

One critic wrote, "Rain reproduces the Beatles' sound so accurately that after a few songs, you will almost believe you are really listening to the four Liverpool lads."

That accuracy is the result of Rain's deep appreciation and knowledge of the Beatles' work. "We really want to be the best at what we do," said Rain member Mark Lewis. "I mean the best anywhere."

Their performances replicate the Beatles' evolution. The first show is a chronological sampling from the three distinct eras of the Beatles' music. The second show is what a Beatles concert might be like, combining earlier and later hits.

The illusion is completed as Rain dons memorable Beatles costumes. Wearing Nehru jackets from the early 1960s, they inspire memories with songs "She Loves You" and "I Want to Hold Your Hand." They revisit the Sgt. Pepper era wearing the satin marching band suits and singing hits such as "Lucy in the Sky With Diamonds." The show's finale pays tribute to the Abbey Road era.

Rain began as most bands do, playing a variety

RAIN: A Tribute to the Beatles.

of music in a variety of clubs. It was during a show several years ago that Rain (then known as Reign) played a rendition of one of the Beatles' better known releases. "The response was so overwhelming that we decided to do only the Beatles," said Lewis.

Rain: A Tribute to the Beatles is made up of Joey Curatolo as Paul, Jim Riddle as John, Joe Bithorn as George and Ralph Castelli as Ringo. For details, call (800) 648-3773 or 788-3773.

St. Romain sizzles at Tahoe Biltmore

St. Romain, featuring Laura St. Romain, will appear in the Savoy Lounge at the Tahoe Biltmore through April 5.

Laura St. Romain hails from an entertainment family. In 1963, her brother, longtime Nevada-area entertainer Kirby St. Romain, scored a hit with "Summer's Coming."

After packing lounges throughout the '70s, Kirby decided to change his act in 1976 and become a comedian. The experiment backfired, and Kirby found himself out of work.

Out of work until his little sister Laura cruised through town with her group, Kansas Rain. The band asked Kirby to hop aboard and he did.

Laura has gone on to make a name for herself in Nevada's clubs.

St. Romain is backed by four other polished musicians: Joe Mendoza bangs the drums; Marc Dyson plays guitar; Russ Litizia of Carson City handles guitar and vocals; and Brian Morgan of Reno lays down the keyboard beat.

St. Romain has been together several years. The band performs a vari-

St. Romain

ety of music, including country, '40s bop, rock 'n' roll and contemporary hits.

There is no cover and no minimum. For show times, call 831-0660.

St. Romain brings music to Harveys

St. Romain entertains in the Casino Theatre Lounge of Harveys Resort Hotel, South Lake Tahoe, through Feb. 28.

Others onstage: Rage Revue for an indefinite engagement, "SinSational Revue" for an indefinite engagement and the Sun Spots through Feb. 28.

Opening in the lounge Feb. 29 is Steppen Stones through March 13 and Big Tiny Little Feb. 29 through March 20.

Show of Power is at the Top of the Wheel Lounge and Restaurant through March 13, along with the Ron Rose Sound for an indefinite engagement.

St. Romain, featuring Laura St. Romain, is a dynamic five-piece band that does a variety of music including country, '40s, rock 'n' roll and contemporary. They do everything from the Temptations to Patti LaBelle and Louis Prima, from Janis Joplin to Patsy Cline.

Joe Mendoz, the drummer, has opened for such acts as Johnny Paycheck and Paul Revere.

Russ Letizia, lead guitarist, also sings lead and background harmonies for St. Romain.

Brian Morgan, keyboard player, encompasses all types of music. He also plays synthesizer, adding horns and strings, and sings lead and background.

BANDING TOGETHER: St. Romain, led by Laura St. Romain, plays at Harveys, South Lake Tahoe, through Feb. 28.

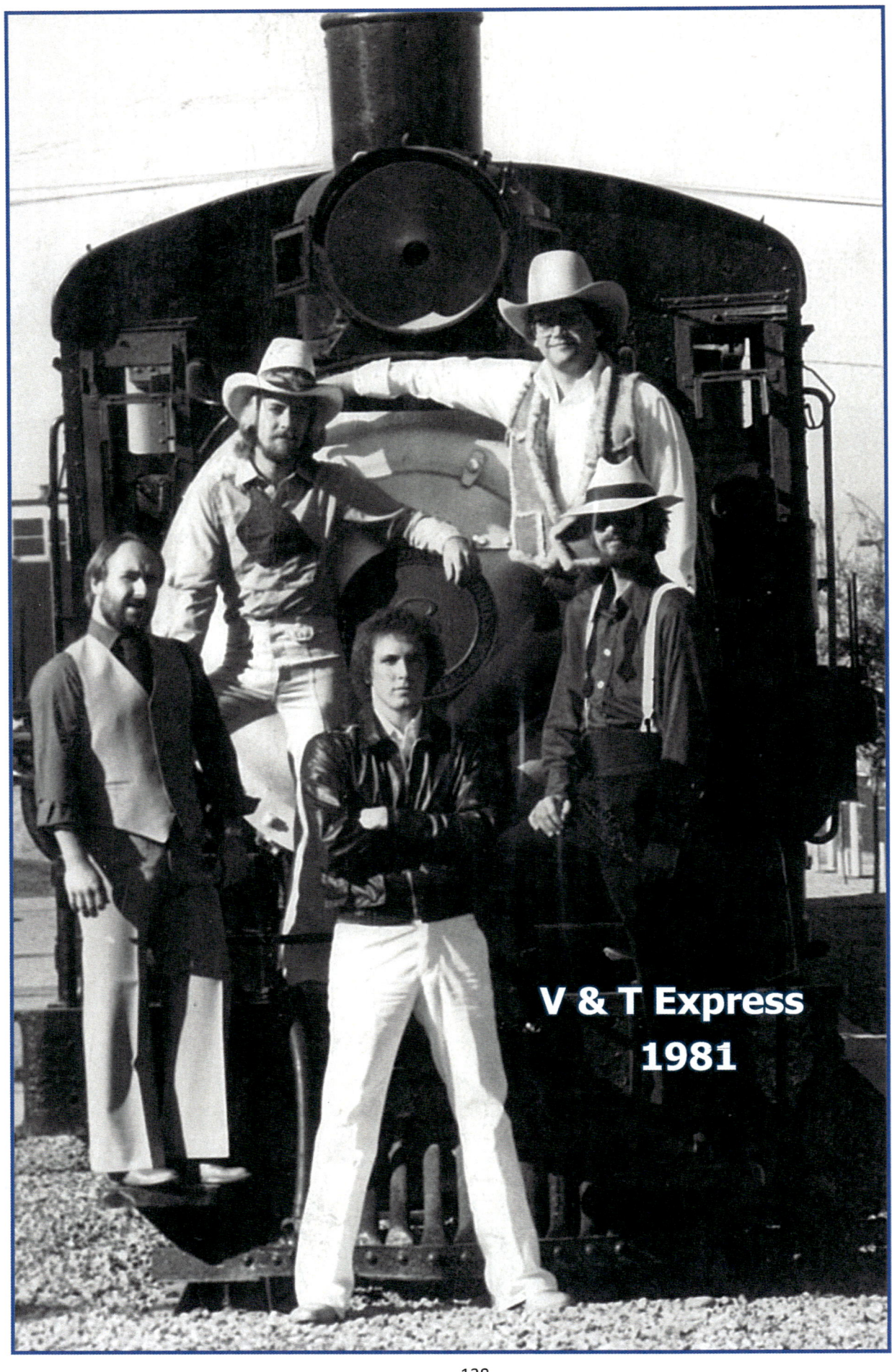

V & T Express
1981

Michael Clark
The Virons

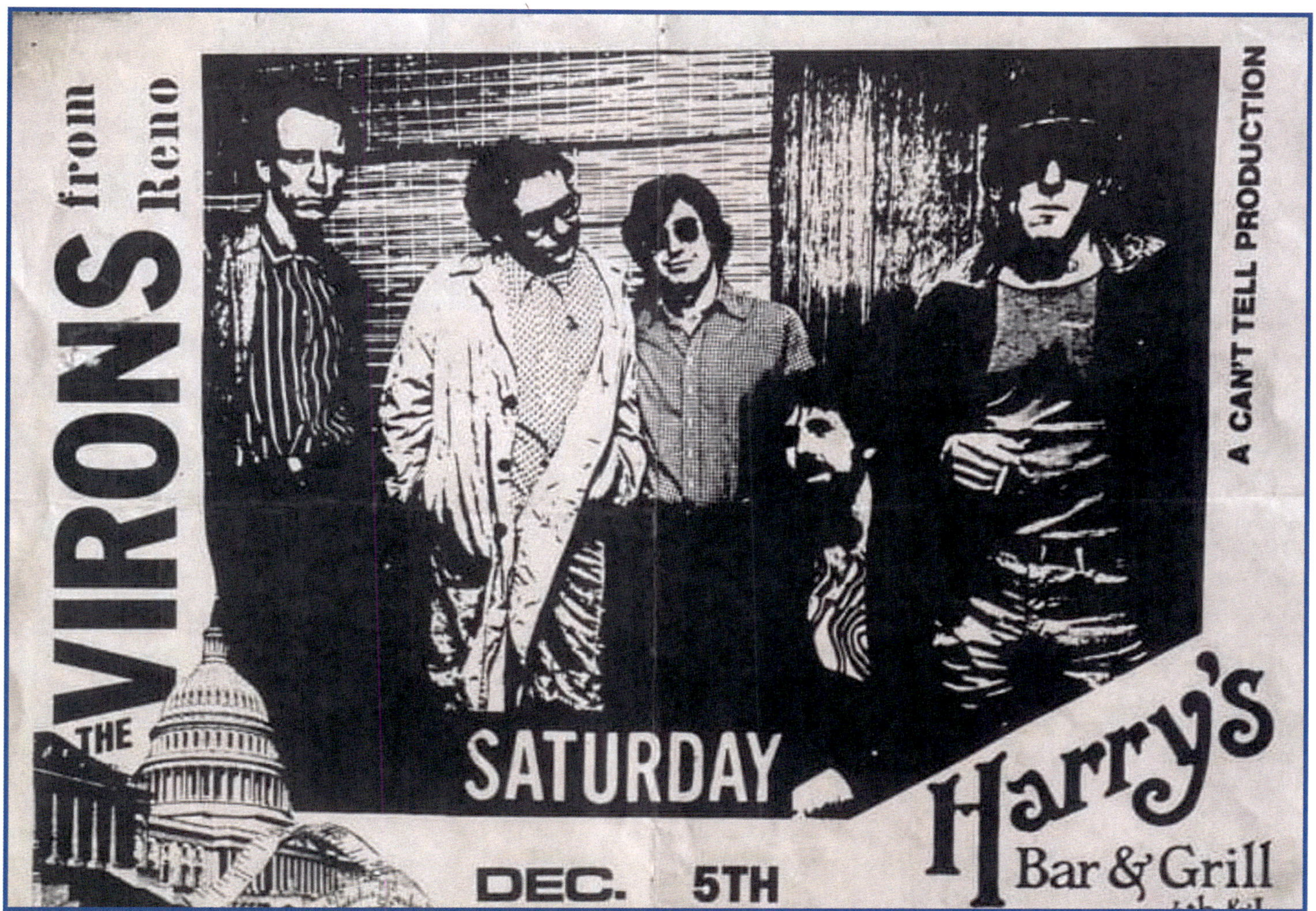
THE VIRONS
from Reno
A CAN'T TELL PRODUCTION
SATURDAY
DEC. 5TH
Harry's
Bar & Grill

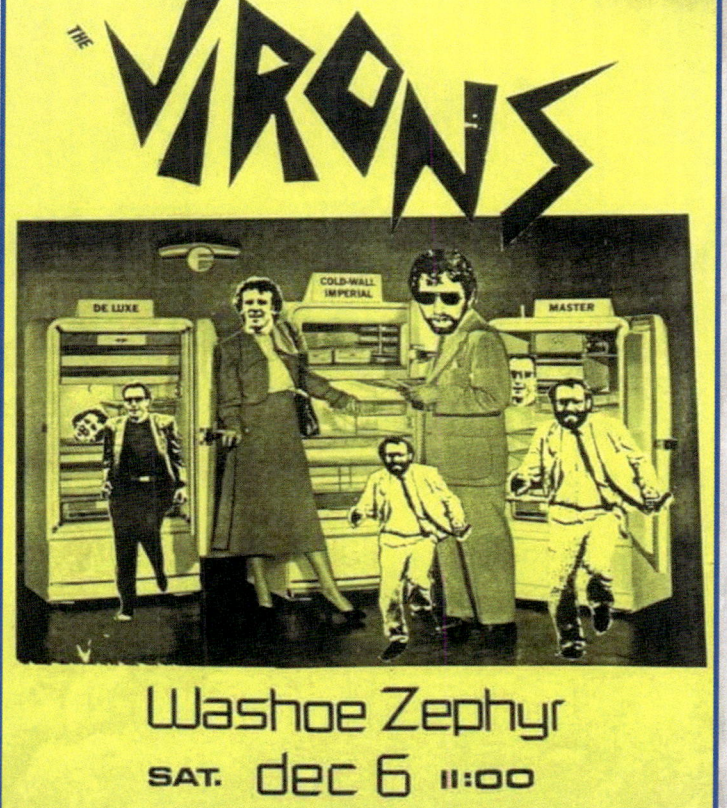

THE VIRONS
DE LUXE
COLD-WALL IMPERIAL
MASTER
Washoe Zephyr
SAT. dec 6 11:00

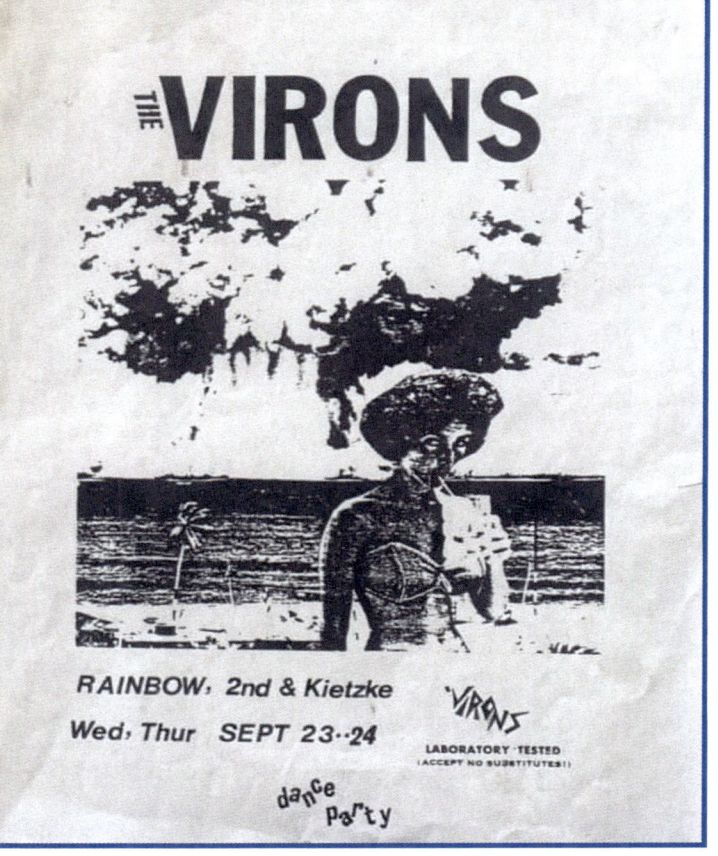

THE VIRONS
RAINBOW, 2nd & Kietzke
Wed, Thur SEPT 23-24
VIRONS
LABORATORY TESTED
(ACCEPT NO SUBSTITUTES!)
dance party

The Svelts, from Sacramento, played Reno often, at The Door, Harrah's, and the American Legion Hall at Tahoe. They went on to become Fanny!

Class of '57 *Presents*

SEPT. 5 — LIVE — COUNTRY WITH **BOBBY DEE**
SEPT. 6 & 7 — OLDIES WITH **BOBBY DEE**

SEPT. 12 — LIVE — COUNTRY WITH **J.C. SILVER**
SEPT. 13 & 14 — OLDIES WITH **STEVIE & THE STRINGRAYS**

SEPT. 19 — LIVE — COUNTRY WITH **RUSH HOUR**
SEPT. 20 & 21 — OLDIES WITH **STAGE DOOR JOHNNY**

SEPT 26 — LIVE — COUNTRY WITH **RUSH HOUR**
SEPT. 27 & 28 — OLDIES WITH **JOHNNY SLICK & THE CHEATERS**

DON'T FORGET THE
CLASS OF '57
WILL CATER TO ALL YOUR
<u>PRIVATE PARTY</u> NEEDS !
3399 N. CARSON ST.   887-1957
NEVER A COVER CHARGE !

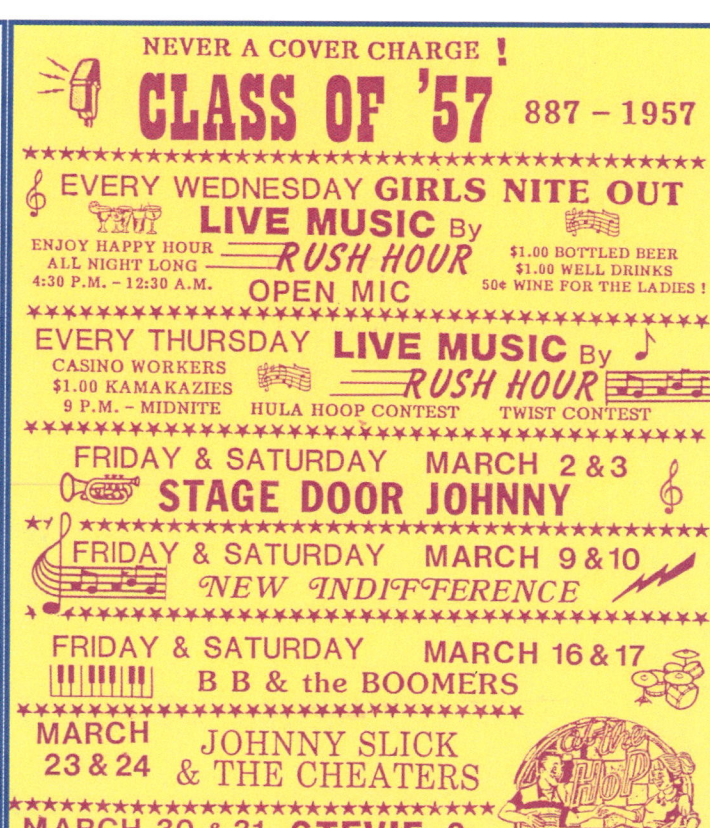

NEVER A COVER CHARGE !
CLASS OF '57   887 - 1957

EVERY WEDNESDAY GIRLS NITE OUT
LIVE MUSIC By *RUSH HOUR*
ENJOY HAPPY HOUR ALL NIGHT LONG
4:30 P.M. - 12:30 A.M.
OPEN MIC
$1.00 BOTTLED BEER
$1.00 WELL DRINKS
50¢ WINE FOR THE LADIES !

EVERY THURSDAY LIVE MUSIC By *RUSH HOUR*
CASINO WORKERS $1.00 KAMAKAZIES 9 P.M. - MIDNITE
HULA HOOP CONTEST   TWIST CONTEST

FRIDAY & SATURDAY   MARCH 2 & 3
STAGE DOOR JOHNNY

FRIDAY & SATURDAY   MARCH 9 & 10
NEW INDIFFERENCE

FRIDAY & SATURDAY   MARCH 16 & 17
B B & the BOOMERS

MARCH 23 & 24   JOHNNY SLICK & THE CHEATERS

MARCH 30 & 31   STEVIE & THE STINGRAYS

3399 N. Carson

Reno rockers, Bill Church and Chuck Ruff with Sammy Hagar and Gary Pihl.

Lost and Found Dept.
1966

Technology interferes with rock concert

By GARY IRATCABAL

Ah, they could have made beautiful music together, Be-Bop Deluxe and Horslips.

But the scourge of mother nature and mechanical problems made Sunday night's concert at the Washoe County Fairgrounds anything but beautiful — or exciting for that matter.

The equipment truck belonging to Horslips broke down somewhere on the other side of Donner Summit, forcing the Irish group to cancel its appearance here. The group, along with Be-Bop Deluxe, had played Winterland in San Francisco the night before.

The fate of the Be-Bop equipment truck paralleled that of the Donner Party, except that Be-Bop managed to solve the snow and mechanical problems which took valuable time.

The equipment arrived in Reno at 6:30 p.m. The concert was to begin at 8.

As roadies worked hard to set up equipment around 7 p.m., lines of people outside the hall began to form. It was cold.

About 9 p.m., the unhappy crowd of around 1,200 began to trickle into the building.

Earlier, rumor had it that a hot local band called Browne Rice was being added to replace Horslips. Other rumors had it that the bass player and lead singer of the group couldn't be reached. How could promoter Michael Schivo (High Sierra Concerts) appear so cool and assured?

Finally, about 9:50 p.m., Browne Rice was assembled on stage in the hall and the show was under way.

The group put out entirely powerhouse rock which contrasted somewhat with what many expected from Be-Bop.

The sound mix was muddy (even taking into account the metal structure of the hall) and the lead singer of the foursome was a little hoarse from a previous engagement.

But Browne Rice has great potential. Currently, the group mixes published material with originals, which is fine for club gigs. The band performed two outstanding Queen songs, "Tie Your Mother Down" and "Stone Coke Crazy," simply blowing the audience away into a rock and roll heavy-metal frame of mind.

This was fine, as English Be-Bop Deluxe followed Browne Rice with a relativly short set — 12 tunes plus encore — that displayed a lot of heavy-metal music.

Granted, there were moments of bloody inspiration as Bill Nelson, the quartet's leader, played a lead guitar that, on one tune called "Shine," from the '77 LP, "Living in the Air Age," ran from a sort of funkadelic to pure and clean hot nit-pickin'.

Nelson proved to be basically the star of the show with his almost Montrose-like style of guitar attack, although keyboard player Andrew Clarke produced some fusion-style leads with electric piano on a song called "Yorkshire Landscape."

CRAZY DANCIN': Crazy 8's headline dance party 6:30 p.m. May 7.

145

Reno Rockers

Danny Quintana

Boris Tavcar

Rod MacKay
1951-2020

Scott Bergstrom
1952-2021

THE COLLINS KIDS

Collector's Edition

The Collins Kids were a nationally-known act who eventually made Reno their home, and appeared at Harrah's often.

Crystal Axe

REVOLVER

Reno
is rocking
August 1-3, 1986

with the most sizzling 50s event ever!

Twist and shout to the classic entertainers of the era

Friday, August 1 Downtown to Reno-Sparks Convention Center
Parade of classic cars
Top entertainment at a fabulous 50s dance
featuring the Coasters, Legends in Concert,
Rocky & The Revellettes
Hosted by Wolfman Jack & Edd "Kookie" Byrnes

Saturday, August 2 — Car show 'n' shine and burnout contest
at Rancho San Rafael
Dance contests — Elvis and Marilyn look-alike contest
Giant concert and dance at Reno-Sparks Convention Center
featuring the Shirelles, Jerry Lee Lewis, Jan & Dean
Del Shannon and The Platters

Sunday, August 3 — Car rally and awards brunch

On your way to or from Expo—take in Reno's 50s Mardi Gras

HOT AUGUST NIGHTS

Sponsored by: Adolph Coors Co. — Eastern Airlines
Great Basin Federal Credit Union
Legends in Concert — Real Properties, Ltd.
Reno Area Hotels & Motels
Reno-Sparks Convention & Visitors Authority
Sunworld Int'l. Airways — Western Airlines

For details & hotel/motel reservations:
Toll Free 1-800-FOR-RENO or in Nevada 702-827-RENO
Telex 170083 or write to
Tourism Department
P.O. Box 837
Reno, NV 89504

The First Year!

1989

CARSON VALLEY INN: Whiskey Ridge romps and stomps to the tune of leader Phil Harris, above, through June 10. KGVM's Captain Buddy plays oldies on Sundays, 7:30 p.m. to midnight. No cover.

1989

HARRAH'S: Lacy J. Dalton.

Wray Brothers
1985

Gary Joe Wade—1980

Music, Smoke-- And Fun

1969

RENO'S BEST TALENT included the "Jonathan Goodlife" band, named a finalist in the "Battle of the Bands" held Friday at the Nevada National Guard Armory. Performing for Reno area teens are lead guitar players, Jerry Werms and James Stipech; drummer, Steve Dunwoodie, and bass guitarist, Terry Peterson. James Mask, organist, is not shown.

(Journal Photo)

Billy Ray Payne - 1965

Steve Hatley - 1965

Justice V - 1967

Rob Hanna

Over a period of 5 decades, Rob Hanna became one of Reno's most popular performers. Initially as a member of several popular groups, he hit his stride with his "Salute to Rod Stewart", taking his show across the country, and to Nova Scotia, Canada, Hawaii, and Guam over a 20-year period.

Hanna at Eldorado

Without a doubt, Rob Hanna is one of the world's best Rod Stewart impersonators and you can catch Hanna and his band, Foolish Behaviour, at the Eldorado Hotel-Casino's Cabaret Dec. 22-31. Hanna looks, sounds and moves like Stewart so it's no surprise that fans confuse him with the pop superstar.

Hanna's play list includes approximately 50 songs and he's always working on new material. He incorporates "Leave Virginia Alone" and "This" from Stewart's latest album, "Spanner in the Works," as well as the classics.

For the "Petty Theft" late show, guitarist Michael Furlong sings lead vocals with Foolish Behaviour as they perform a variety of Tom Petty tunes. These talented musicians cover a number of Petty's hits including "Learning to Fly," "Free Fallin'" and "I Won't Back Down."

Rob with Foolish Behaviour in Oklahoma City, 1984. (The girls were the promoter's daughters)

1983

Rob Hanna's
salute to
Rod Stewart

Marriott's Great America
Knott's Berry Farm
Santa Clara County Fair
Harrah's—Tahoe & Reno
The Dunes—Las Vegas
The 1982 East Coast Fair Tour

Rob Hanna, a look-alike, sound-alike Rod Stewart, will appear Thursday, May 13, at Cabo's (co-sponsored by KFM radio) with a five-piece band. Also appearing will be the comedy group Man Over Board and Chico rockers Model Citizens. Hanna returns to Cabo's May 14, Friday night, with two shows. Also appearing will be Model Citizens. If you want to see a great impersonation of Stewart, don't miss Hanna's show.

BROOK BRIGHT

STEVE HATLEY

JERRY COLEMAN

All my best Rob Hanna '85

ROB HANNA

salute to ROD STEWART

MARK CAMPBELL

with FOOLISH BEHAVIOR

PAUL MANKTELOW

Innovative Entertainment, Inc.

1401 Shore Street
West Sacramento, CA 95691

P. O. Box 60845
Sacramento, CA 95860

(916) 442-6983 • 973-0909

159

ROB? ROD? ROB . . .: Rob Hanna does his Rod Stewart tribute so convincingly, "People ask me for my autograph all the time," he says. "Sometimes I explain, sometimes I don't and I go ahead and sign my name." Hanna and his band, Foolish Behaviour, play the Eldorado Cabaret through March 21. The band's lead guitarist, Michael Furlong, keeps the fun going with his "Reflections of Tom Petty." For show times, call (800) 648-5966 or 786-5700.

High Sierra spotlights 'Lipstick,' Rob Hanna and Frenz

World-famous stripper Tempest Storm is a rare phenomenon in the world of entertainment. For more than 30 years she's been captivating audiences with her exotic strip-tease artistry and today she remains the best in the business.

"The Last Superstar of Burlesque" is the star of the revue "Lipstick" playing an indefinite run in the Pine Cone Lounge at Del Webb's High Sierra Casino-Hotel.

Rob Hanna brings his popular "Salute to Rod Stewart" to the Pine Cone Lounge Dec. 9-10. In Lily's Dance Hall, Frenz plays a frenzy of tunes through Dec. 18.

"Lipstick," an adult revue-burlesque production, is a fast-paced mix of provocative dance numbers, sensational costumes and the comedy of multi-talented impressionist Bethany Owen. Her comic routine includes impressions of stars such as Barbra Streisand, Cher, Carol Channing, Jane Fonda, Diana Ross, Tina Turner and Joan Rivers.

Headliner Tempest Storm has always been known for her tasteful and elegant strip act. After "taking it off" for some 36 years, the red-headed bombshell is still as dazzling as ever — and shows no signs of slowing down. "I love my work and I'm very dedicated," she says.

Tempest, who grew up Annie Blanche Banks, was born into a sharecropping family in a small Georgia town. After escaping a violent and deprived home life she managed to land a job as a chorus dancer in Hollywood's Follies Theater. She made her first deal to

Hanna   Frenz

strip while dancing in order to pay for extensive dental work.

Tempest plans to reveal some of her secrets for her enduring youth in an upcoming book. She says the idea to write the book actually came from her female fans. "Women give me so many compliments," she says. "They tell me I'm an inspiration to them and they want to know how I do it. It's very flattering."

Just last year Tempest published her autobiography, "The Lady is a Vamp," a sizzling account of her struggle to the top. With her renewed notoriety Tempest now plans to pursue a role in a nighttime soap opera.

Rob Hanna, a native of northern Nevada, has been

studying and perfecting his Rod Stewart routine for years. He's got the Stewart look, moves and music refined into an art — and is even mistaken for Stewart off stage.

Frenz, playing in Lily's Dance Hall, is a multi-talented musical ensemble that had its beginnings in Detroit in the late '70s. After extensive auditions, leader Steven Cowart brought together a group of top musicians.

Frenz offers a repertoire of styles ranging from the harmonic vocal sounds of the '40s and '50s, to the soft and hard rock sounds of today.

Frenz is a versatile, high energy and entertaining musical unit. For show times, call 588-6211.

SECONDS
C O U N T

Punk band 7 Seconds has bloomed from its Reno roots

By Michael Sion
GAZETTE-JOURNAL

If there were such a thing as a Reno Rock 'n' Roll Hall of Fame, Steve Youth would be in it.

His punk band, 7 Seconds, made it out of area clubs in the '80s to grab a big-label record deal.

The feat was a first, and remains unique, say local music observers.

"We made it a point to go out and spread our music," Youth says of his band, which began in 1980 as a bunch of adolescents thrashing three chords with fury.

"On our first tour, we traveled in a 1958 Volkswagen bus. We didn't care. We wanted to do it."

Bassist Youth, a.k.a. Steve Marvelli, is now 27. Brother Kevin, the singer-songwriter, is 31. Drummer Troy Mowat, from South Lake Tahoe, is 29. And guitarist Bobby Adams — who joined in '86 when 7 Seconds' career was in full swing — is 24.

They've had their ups and downs. Toured with the Circle Jerks and other underground "name" bands. Played Europe and across the states — from New York's CBGB to the Outhouse, a club in a Kansas cornfield.

They've been tattooed. Bleary-eyed. Broken up. Burned — they say — by their old record label, Restless, a subsidiary of Enigma.

Now the band's reformed, going full-throttle since August and ready to burst from Reno again with an album to be released at summer's end for a San Diego independent label, Cargo.

Promoter Ben Wilcox recalls 7 Seconds from its heyday.

"Their energy and charisma out on stage is still there," says Wilcox, 24.

"It's in-your-face material. If they would've had good management, five or six years ago, they probably would've been Pearl Jam or Nirvana."

7 Seconds began after the Sex Pistols and other seminal punk bands inspired Youth and brother Steve to pick up instruments.

"We were destined to be musicians," says Youth. "Our mother was a hippie."

The other two founders were brothers Tom and Jimmy Froines. 7 Seconds' first tape was titled "3 Chord Politics." One of their singles was "Socially ——— Up."

The band name meant nothing. It was just short and snappy.

In 1980, there was no Reno club for punks to play. But there was "the Rat House," a home off Montello Street with a back room converted into a playroom. Some older players rented it, and big underground bands showed up: the Dead Kennedys, Black Flag.

"People naturally assumed every band was singing racist, violent stuff," Youth says. "For the most part, hard-core was against that sort of thing."

7 Seconds made a bit of money and hit the road. Sacramento. Fresno. "There was a place down down in San Francisco called the Mabuhay Gardens that we started playing," says Youth, who dropped out of Hug High School.

7 Seconds' first full-length album came out in '84, on the minor BYO label. A 15-year-old Bobby Adams bought it, got a cheap guitar at Bizarre Guitar, learned to play to the tape.

By '86, he was in the band.

Tough times followed. There wasn't much money in the punk scene. Youth toiled in an eatery at Reno-Cannon International Airport. His hair hung down his back. He hacked it off.

Soon after, he got an audition with Metallica — the top-level metal band. Youth said he made it to the final three to be the band's new bassist. He thinks his shorn locks held him back.

But now there's 7 Seconds' new record deal. A tour is shaping up to take the band back to Europe and across the United States, playing colleges, small clubs and halls.

It's more melodic than ever.

"We've been called the Beach Boys of punk rock, by Soundgarden," Youth says, referring to the Seattle metal band.

7 Seconds now pens only positive songs, says Youth. One is "Happy Rain," about Brazilian subway surfers — train-top riders.

"It's good fun music, it's anti-violence," says Youth. "Our singer's a Buddhist."

---

7 Seconds headlines an all-ages show that begins at 4 p.m. (gate opens at 3) Sunday at the Icehouse Saloon, 310 Spokane St. Tickets are $8. Details: 786-8858.

Also slated are three Reno acts: Grumple, BOHJ, War Maggots.

Floyd Rose

Greg Golden

♪ ECLIPSE ♫

Dennis Collins

Lou Werlinger

Who Am I, Anyway?
By Artist/Musician Paul D. Manktelow

If you were fortunate enough to be a teenager in the mid-60's, you probably remember a time of love, sunshine, and flowers in your hair. The world had suddenly changed, and a lot of that change was due to the music that floated out over the airwaves called "The British Invasion". I was about sixteen at that time, just a young English bloke with a strange accent, a guitar slung over my shoulder, and hair that hung down over my collar. I was a part of that movement and had just landed in Reno. I suddenly found myself thrust up on stage at the State Building, playing for a thousand kids rockin' and rollin' the night away, flying high on the wings of music. I had somehow been cast into Reno's most prominent band, the Justus V. Those glory days didn't last but a couple of years, but they will always be remembered as some of the best times of my life.

After a short stint in the armed forces, due to unfortunate circumstances, I found myself living in Vancouver, British Columbia. By that time, my musical interest had changed to more acoustic guitar playing and writing songs. During this time I was occasionally visited by old musician friends and band members from Reno and the Bay Area. One memorable time was when Ronnie Montrose, Steve Hatley, and Bill Church came to visit. They had just finished the album "Sawbuck" for Fillmore Records (Bill Graham's label) and were given a retainer. They used the money to drive up to Canada and visit me, and we shared some amazing jam sessions and good times together.

"Good times, bad times, you know I've had my share"... At this point in my life my interests had evolved, and I decided to make a career change and give up music to become an artist. I spent 1972 bicycling around Europe, painting landscapes and selling them to finance my trip. In 1973 I moved back to England, set up a studio, and continued scraping out a living from my paintings, but soon the music bug came and bit me on the ass and I joined the well-known folk group "Plumb Duff", formerly "The Mariners". This was a totally new and informative experience for me...learning through old English folk songs about the roots of my British homeland.

The band was very entertaining on stage, too...storytelling, joking around, and acting the fools, often breaking into song "a capella" in public places such as elevators, markets, and restaurants. We were most busy playing scores of pubs on the English folk scene around the south of England, and also did a tour of Belgium. This was a very influential experience for me.

After a few years in England, I returned to Canada and lived in Victoria, B.C. to pursue my art career, and became quite successful with my fantasy art. When things were just starting to bloom, the music bug came and bit me on the ass again, and I formed the band "Amazon Grace", a rockin' little three-piece band, doing mostly my original songs. The band was making a good name for themselves and doing well until we were booked into a Prince Rupert cabaret in Northern Canada by Head First Productions (Mike and Kathie Mantor's agency in Reno). After playing one night the hotel caught on fire and burned to the ground, destroying most of our equipment. We barely escaped with our lives, and unfortunately "Amazon Grace" never recovered. After this disaster I decided to do a folk group like the one I'd played with in England ("Plumb Duff"). I moved back to Reno and created "Sailor's Farm". We played locally on a small scale in Truckee, Northstar, etc., and were named band of the year at the Blue Mail Box in Reno.

As time moved on I joined forces with other Reno musicians and played with such bands as "Bandana", and "Wilder Street". Head First Productions kept us busy playing every weekend for about three or four years. "Wilder Street" played a lot at well-known venues like the Town House and the Grand Ballroom. Reno was really rockin' at that time, and I eventually ended up in "Rob Hanna's Salute to Rod Stewart", which was another life-changing experience as we were constantly on the road throughout America, Canada, and Mexico. After that, I played as a solo artist and made a CD of some of my original songs, called "Sturdy Beggar". I went on to form my final band, "The Sturdy Beggars", a Celtic-style band in which I was able to return to my English roots once again.

"Dreams come true,
and some fall thru".

Nowadays, as I'm "sitting in my English Garden, waiting for the sun", I think to myself "what a long, strange trip it's been'. I have enjoyed every moment of it. Cheers!

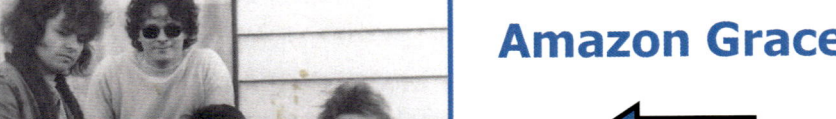

Amazon Grace

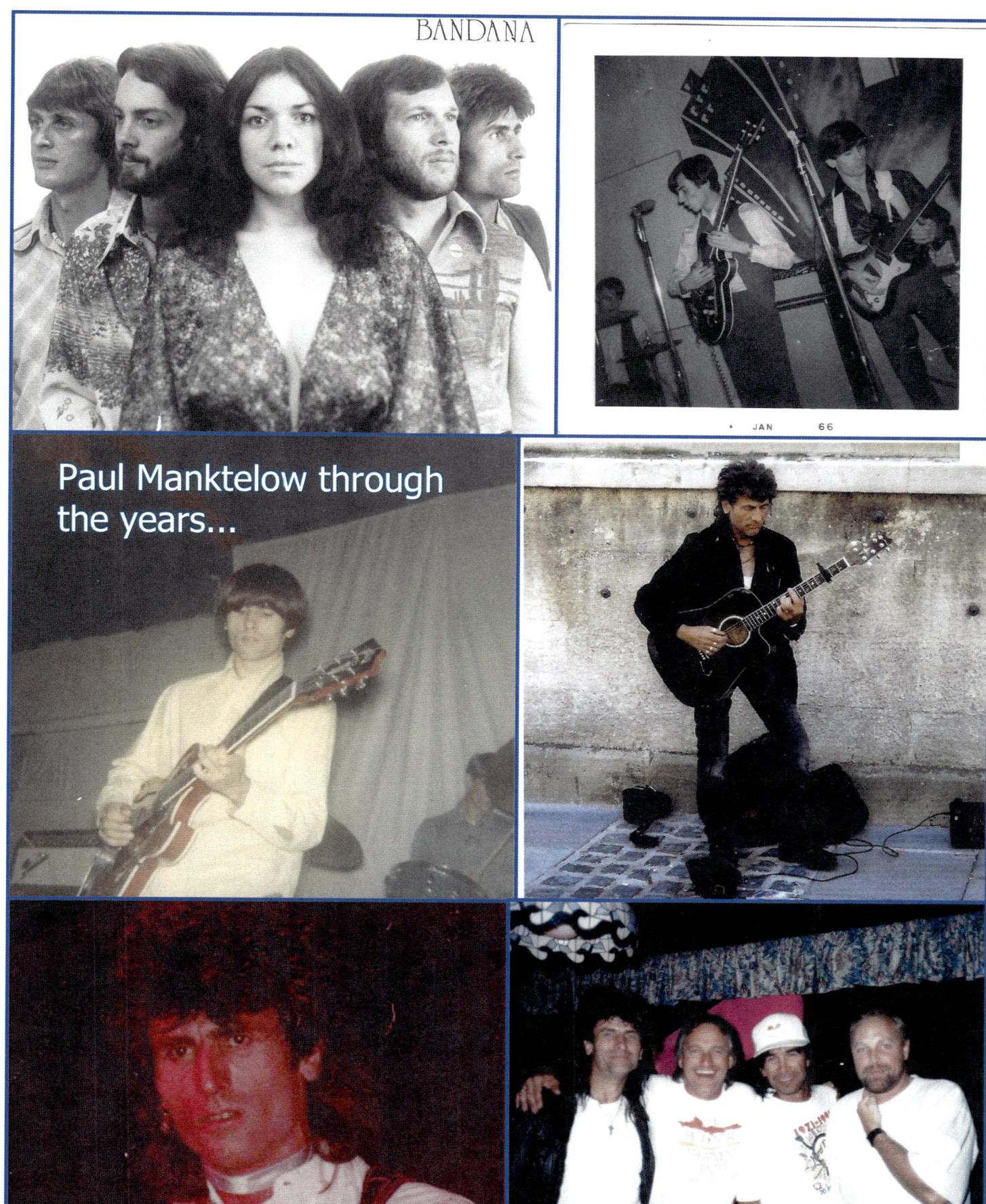

BANDANA

Paul Manktelow through the years...

JAN 66

It's not so hot being a 'hot' band

Firemen breaking window at rear of building.

A Victoria rock-band's first road-trip ended in near-disaster last week when the Prince Rupert hotel at which they were playing burned down on the second day of their projected two-week stay.

Although the four musicians, members of a three-month-old group called Amazon Grace, escaped unhurt from the blaze last Tuesday morning at the New Royal Hotel, most of their personal belongings did not.

Left stranded and virtually penniless, they could not recover any money for the Victoria return flight from the hotel owner or obtain any help from welfare and so had to borrow money from the drummer's parents to pay the airline.

Lead guitar Paul Manktelow said Saturday the group had done one night's work at the hotel when it was gutted by fire the following morning.

Although staying on the third floor in separate rooms the four musicians managed to scramble for safety from the smoke-filled building.

However Manktelow noted that lead-singer Doug Goddard had to be pulled out from the hotel lobby "by his hair."

Back in Victoria the group is awaiting delivery of its equipment salvaged from the water-logged cabaret in the hotel's basement.

It is also looking into the question of obtaining legal aid to help recover money owed them by the hotel.

The story however had its bright side and Manktelow noted that it "wasn't a total loss, it really brought the band together in lots of ways."

He also said he had spoken to their agent who told him: "We heard you were a really

hot group but we didn't ... you were this hot."

There were an estimat... people in the hotel at the ... of the fire but only one ... suffered any injury. He ... his ankle when forced to ... from the second storey.

Plum Duff, 1972
Paul Manktelow, 2nd from left

Sailor's Farm

Wilder Street

LOCAL folk group Plum Duff have just returned from a successful short tour of Belgium before embarking on a full trans-Europe trek early next year.

The group played three club dates in Belgium and the response has left the members in confident mood for the forthcoming tour of Holland, Belgium, Luxembourg and Germany in April.

Plum Duff has only been around for nine months and is rapidly establishing itself as one of the most promising newcomers to the folk scene.

Leader of the outfit is John Towner, a name and face familiar to many as a former member of the popular Mariners group whose album Best of Folk recently topped the 40,000 sales mark.

MANDOLIN

In Plum Duff he handles the vocals and plays guitar, mandolin, autoharp and whistle and is joined by Reg Marchant from Westfield, Colin Baldwin from Hailsham, Phil Ratcliffe from Staplehurst and Paul Manktalow.

The group is about to suffer the blow of losing Hastings-born Paul, however, as he is set to return to America, where he has spent most of his life, next month.

There is a replacement already lined-up in the shape of another ex-Mariner, fiddler Gary Blakeley who has recently left music college.

In addition to the European tour, Plum Duff also have plans for an album and cassette in the pipeline and they were in action recently at the Black Horse where they are one of the resident groups.

Super success for talented Plum Duff

● Plum Duff — a great tour.

ENGLISH bluegrass comes to the Black Horse, Telham, tonight when the guests are Mountain Line.

Plenty of British folk influence has been melted with the American music to give the outfit a distinctly Anglicised brand of country music.

The group grew up out of Western Line and Mountain Dew and their present line-up reads: Pat Mathe, mandolin, Barry Mathe, guitar, Jim Brookes, banjo, Mick Hughes, bass, and Ian McCann, fiddle and guitar.

Paul Manktelow

An Evening with
"The Sturdy Beggar"
Saturday, November 25th

Celebrating his New CD
at "THE JIB"
at the Marina in Sparks
8:00pm - 10:00pm

1991

Paul Manktelow was summoned to Nashville to portray Keith Richards in Alan Jackson's video for "Don't Rock the Jukebox", which featured the line "my heart's not ready for the Rollin' Stones". The gentleman on the right is Hal Smith, who was also in the video. Mr. Smith is best remembered as Otis, the town drunk, on "The Andy Griffith Show".

1965

Today

1965

Paul Manktelow in his Justus V uniform jacket.

Fifty-eight years, and it still fits!

Johnny Slick and The Cheaters

Johnny Slick and The Cheaters

SILVER DOLLAR LOUNGE PRESENTS
ROCK + ROLL AT ITS BEST

RUSTY BUTZ

Two!! Action Packed Weeks!

ONLY $1.00 at door
I.D. required

Nov. 20, 21, 22 — 27, 28, 29

LOU'S VILLAGE PROUDLY PRESENTS

LOS HUEVOS

9 pm
Friday ~ July 31

Here's the handy dandy little wonder that doesn't slice, dice or grate carrots!

SATURDAY AT THE DOGHOUSE MAY 16th

9:30 IF WE'RE LATE... START WITHOUT US

This Summer...
rock & roll

WITH MILESTONE

COMBINED SILVER CITY DAYTON
at the DAYTON Ballfield
Sat. Sept. 4
7:00pm - 1:00am
$6.00
$10.00 couple

FIREMEN'S BALL
FEATURING
SUTRO
ALL STARS
DECOYS
HARD BARGAIN

Ticket Give Away

Los Huevos

NEVADA BAND

NEW YEARS EVE PARTY with MILESTONE

MINDEN INN DEC. 28-29 31

BIG WET T-shirt! CONTEST

MILESTONE

MINDEN INN AUG. 31 SEPT. 1

Get an earful

GEORGE'S rock & roll GEORGE'S in Carson City finally

GEORGE'S PRESENTS MILESTONE

OCT. 5-6 10:00 You've got to hear it to believe it

Lou Werlinger

Rusty Butz...Butts!

Rusty Butz

177

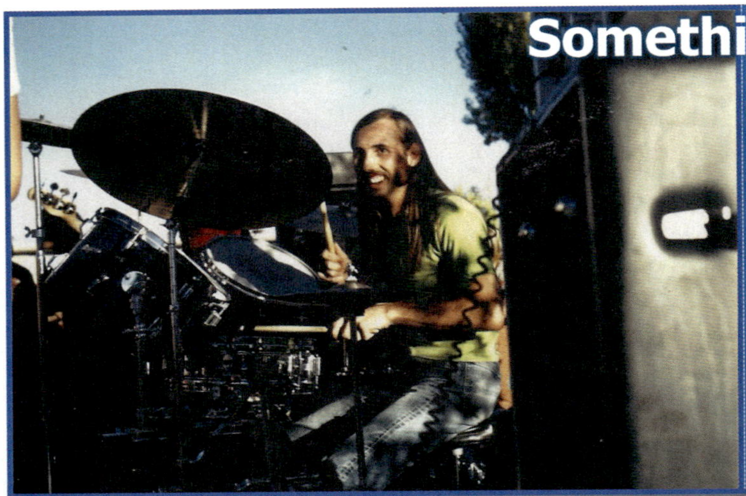
Something Nasty

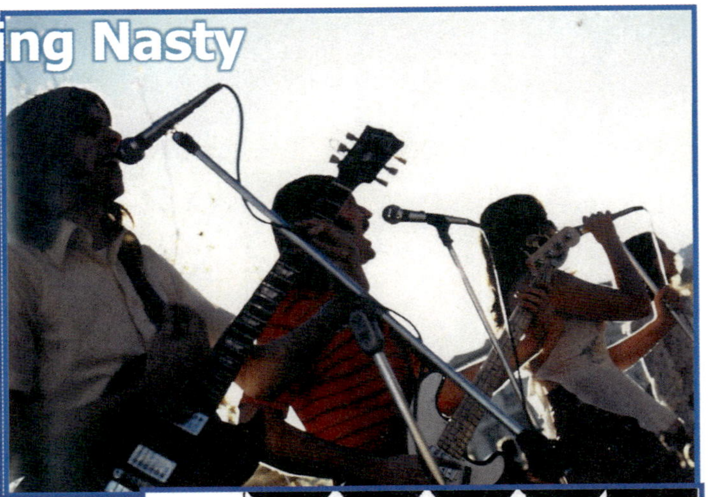

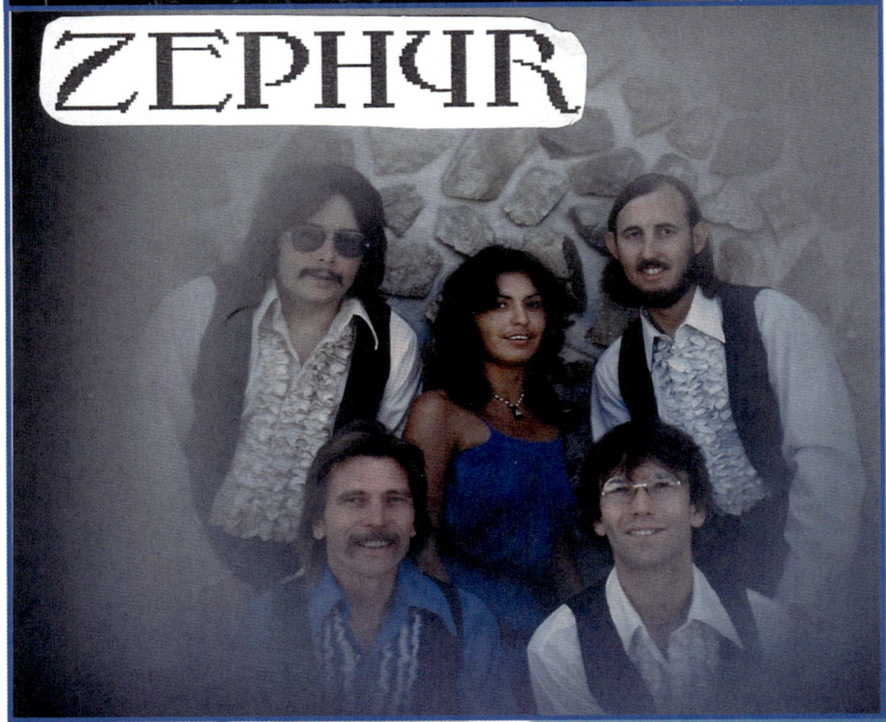
ZEPHYR

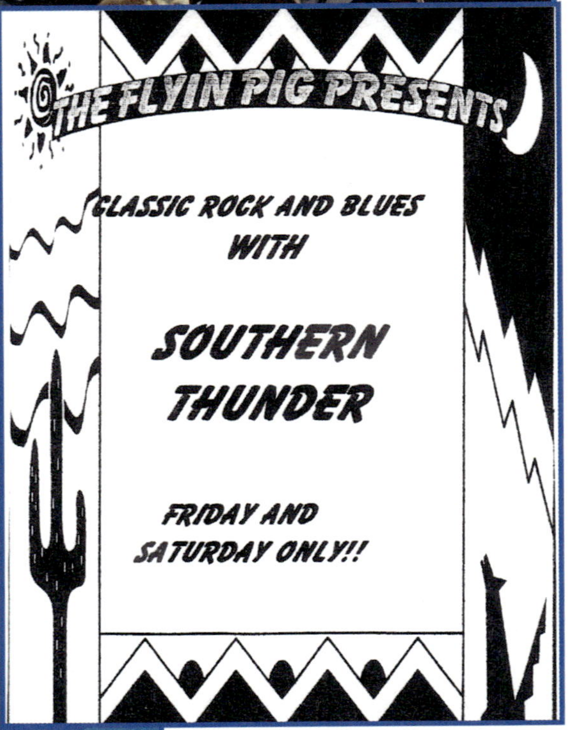
THE FLYIN PIG PRESENTS
CLASSIC ROCK AND BLUES
WITH
SOUTHERN
THUNDER
FRIDAY AND
SATURDAY ONLY!!

Southern Thunder

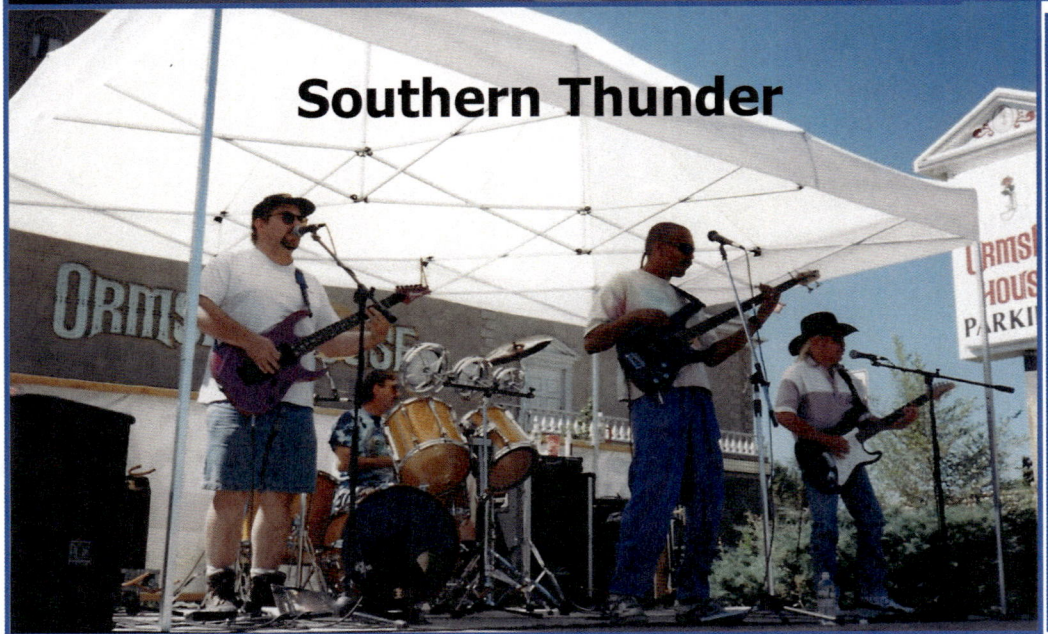

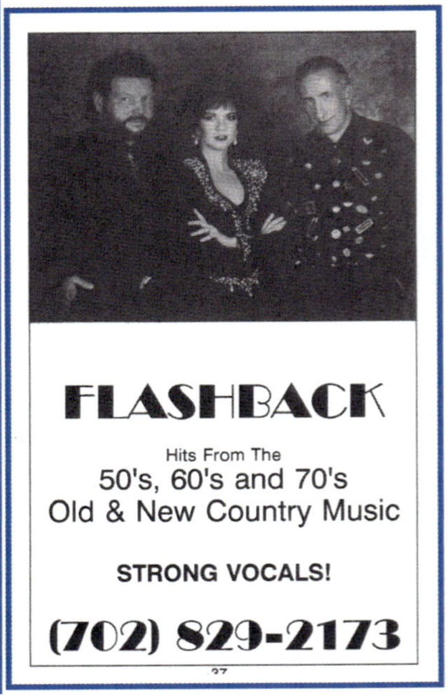
FLASHBACK
Hits From The
50's, 60's and 70's
Old & New Country Music
STRONG VOCALS!
(702) 829-2173

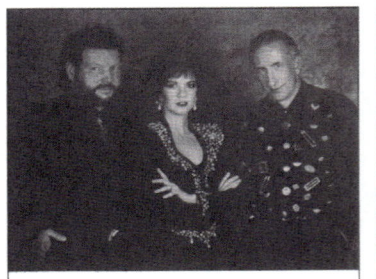

RED DAWN

STILL CRUZIN'

The Decoys

Teen Center Holds First Rock Dance

The Nevada Appeal was an unwitting "supporter" of the arts last Saturday night as the Teen Center held its first dance.

Approximately 170 teenagers showed up for the event which members of the sponsoring Carson Jaycees hope will be held on a weekly basis.

Performing were two local Rock groups, The Chosen Few and The Chipped Beef on Toast.

A platform for the musicians was improvised using thousand pound rolls of Nevada Appeal newsprint paper as a base.

The center is also open weekdays between six and 10

CHIPPED BEEF ON TOAST

Brother Me

...ured at Joe Pruett's Mint Club in Carson City are the ...er Me," a highly accepted rock group consisting of five ...usicians and a girl lead singer. They play on a Wed. thru ...ht schedule.

Rusty Butz

Naunie Furlong

Rusty Butz, a new name for a number of fine local musicians who have been gaining a top following locally, will be repeating this weekend at Gene Schwartz' Carson Hot Springs. Appearing Friday and Saturday is the group which was formed from Albany, Double Down and Eclipse, and who have just finished a tour of five Western states — California, Oregon, Utah, Montana and Idaho. They are composed of Bill Campbell, base; Ray Rodarte, guitar; Nauni Furlong, vocals; Lou Werlinger, drums, and Mike Furlong, guitar. They specialize in Boogie Rock. Gene said that they will be followed by the popular Sutro Sympathy Orchestra in the continuing Hot Springs program of weekend entertainment.

Kandas Myer with "Baba Tao"
Whitaker Park, July 4, 1976

2nd Coming

1973

HEIDI WILSON

Peppermill

Peppermill

HEIDI WILSON

183

Heidi Wilson Band

Sound

Sound Factor, a Reno-based group, plays music from old standards to intricate rock tunes at Chuck's Golden Spike in Carson City through Feb. 20. Opening Feb. 22 is the Denny Long Duo.

Harmonizing

The Denny Long duo harmonizes on a variety of styles as Long plays drums and blues harmonica while Doug Cecil strums guitar at Chuck's Golden Spike in Carson City through March 13. The duo plays country, rock, folk and old standards.

It may have been a lucky break

RON BUTLER

A broken neck took Ron Butler off the gridiron and put him on the stage. Butler, who appears through January 29th in the Onslow Hotel's Supper Club, was playing center for the Detroit Lions when the accident occurred.

Butler had always faced a conflict between body and mind. From the time he entered high school as a 6'3", 215-pound freshman, he wanted to sing.

"But the high school coach took one look at me and decided I should play ball. "It's strange a kid your size wanting to sing," the coach told me as he drafted me into football. My favorite subject was always choir," Butler says.

Football provided a scholarship to the University of Colorado where Butler graduated with a BA in Business. He was drafted by the Denver Broncos and spent a year with that club before the fateful move to the Detroit Lions.

It was during an exhibition game against the Kansas City Chiefs that center Butler abruptly ended his career.

"I didn't really like football," Butler confesses. "The only reason I played was to help my music career. You'd be surprised how many doors it opens."

So when his football career ended Butler was ready to pick up his guitar and devote himself to his first love — music.

"I enjoy myself when I'm working," he says. "Anyone who gets bored on stage is not an entertainer."

Of course any alternative to being fallen on, pummeled and bitten by Mean Joe Greene is heaven.

Kenny Rost Kenny Lowrey   Jack Farell Tommy Roscoe

The

Country Playboys

1974

July 1969

Del Mar Station

Invites You To an Evening with

L.A. GUNS

with Special Guest

Crystal Axe

Monday, January 29, 1996

Tickets
$15.00 + $1.00 surcharge
$17.00 at the door
available at:
Del Mar Station
Mirabelli's
Shea's Tavern

Del Mar will be selling Hot Dogs
and Nachos

Doors opens at 8 p.m.
Show starts at 8:30 p.m.

R O C K   D I V A

Reno Live presents
JOAN JETT
and the Blackhearts

O N   T O U R   N O W

with Special Guests
Sledd & Local 420

Saturday, October 9, 1999
Reno Live
45 W. Second St., Reno, Nevada 89501

Doors Open at 7:00 p.m.
$22.00 - Adv.
$25.00 - Day of Show
21 & Over

Ticket Outlets:
Reno Live Ph: 329-1952
JJ's Ear Candy, Carson Ph: 885-8863
Mirabelli's PH: 825-7210
Recycled Records PH: 826-4119

BLACKHEART RECORDS

THE BEST OF RENO IX   1989

Gary Wade & The Bump

READER FAVORITES: Although Washoe County District Attorney Mills Lane, regularly top vote-getter at the local public official, doesn't appear to agree, readers picked Gary Wade & the Bump the Reno-Sparks area's best local band and Wade himself its best local musician.

WADE BROTHERS DAY - 1985

FREE CONCERT

IN
PARADISE PARK
SAT. AUG. 31ST

AT THE "OLD RENO ARCH" NEAR ODDIE BLVD & SILVERADA

MUSIC STARTS AT 2 P.M.

BE A PART OF A LIVE VIDEO AND AUDIO RECORDING WITH THE WADE BROTHERS & BILLY HILL BAND AND SPECIAL GUESTS.

PROCEEDS FROM CONCESSIONS BENEFIT "MARCH OF DIMES"

NO ALCOHOLIC BEVERAGES PLEASE

BEER, WINE COOLERS SOFT DRINKS & FOOD WILL BE SOLD AT THE EVENT.

Special Thanks to

MORREY DISTRIBUTORS • STARSOUND AUDIO • GUARANTEED MARKETING
DUKE'S STEAK HOUSE • SIERRA NEVADA JOB CORPS RANGERS • PEPSI COLA
KOZZ 105 FM • TRANSPORTATION SERVICES, INC. • CONTEMPO TV 55
FROGGY'S LUNCH BOX

March of Dimes
BIRTH DEFECTS FOUNDATION

"Fiver"—1976
(first incarnation)

James Cavanaugh and The Charm of Hugo

Jay Ramsey Band plays Sahara

Jay Ramsey is known in music and entertainment circles for two main reasons. . .first, as the lead singer of an award-winning show group, and second, as a million-selling songwriter for such artists as Elvis Presley, Roy Clark and Conway Twitty.

Now, these entertaining and creative forces have been brought together in and exciting new fusion. . .the Jay Ramsey Band, playing through August 7 in the Pine Cone Lounge of the Sahara Tahoe.

As founding partner and lead singer in the highly acclaimed show band, Expression, Ramsey has spent the past several years entertaining audiences throughout the U.S.

Now, he has built his latest band around former Expression members Frank Cole and Mack Clayton, while adding widely experienced musicians Tony Smith and John Leach.

The result is a hard driving band which entertains with pop, country and crossover music, while adding a very personal dimension, the original compositions of Jay Ramsey.

Big Frank Cole is a noted sax stylist who doubles, triples and more on several instruments. He and Ramsey have played together for years, and their closeness is evident in the controlled energy of their vocal harmonies.

Mack Clayton, another former Expression member is drummer for the group, playing a powerful, yet understated style.

Newcomers Smith and Leach can play keyboards, brass and reeds while providing extra vocal ammunition.

The Jay Ramsey Band brings their power-packed sound to the Sahara Tahoe nightly through August 7.

KENNY STAHL AND FRIENDS

BRENT ZANE

JOHN WHEELER

KENNY STAHL

AND FRIENDS

Kenny Stahl plays flutes, saxophones, piano, organ and bass. In the music world, Kenny is a well-known jazz flautist from Miami, Florida. Besides being one of the original Muscle Shoals Horns, Kenny has an impressive record of studio work, symphony performances and guest appearances at national music clinics on the east coast.

****

Since moving west in 1973, he has accumulated a long list of successful engagements including *Harrahs, Harolds Club, North Shore Club* and various other major hotels including *The Sheraton, Holiday Inn, Hyatt House* and *Howard Johnsons* circuits.

****

With his unique style, Kenny is acknowledged by many as being one of the finest flautists in the United States. Using his many keyboards for a full and versatile sound, Kenny's high energy lead vocals and saxophones add a new dimension to the basic trio format.

John Wheeler is on electric and acoustic guitars, pedal steel, bass guitar and vocals. John was born in London, England and has worked extensively throughout Europe. He spent two years as a session musician for Saga Records in London and performed on cruise ships for Sitmar Lines. He then moved to Australia and joined one of that countrys top concert and recording groups.

Since arriving in the U.S. four years ago, John has worked with many well-known groups and cabaret shows.

Brent Zane is on drums, percussion and vocals. Also a studio session musician, Brent has had extensive professional experience performing in many major concerts and cabarets throughout the U.S. and Canada. Brent is an extremely versatile drummer, awarded in symphonic and rudimental percussion.

Kenny Stahl and Friends have acquired a large repertoire enabling them to perform any style of music from dinner sets to rock and roll, disco or high-energy show and dance revues.

With this combination of talent and experience, *Kenny Stahl and Friends* have become one of Nevada's top drawing attractions.

Brent zane   Kenny Stahl   John Wheeler

Vocal harmonies are their strength

"Cleveland" is appearing indefinately in Leo's Lair at the MGM Grand in Reno.

This versatile group specializes in vocal harmonies in many styles. Sometimes they remind listeners of "The Four Freshmen," or the "Mills Brother," at other times they recall "Alabama," "The Beach Boys" or Tom Jones.

Glenn Williams leads the group with his rich voice and guitar and banjo talents. Mike Sankovich plays keyboards, Dave Sifritt is on bass and Will Kinsey takes the drums.

"Cleveland" has often performed in Reno, Lake Tahoe and Las Vegas in recent years.

CLEVELAND

The Decoys

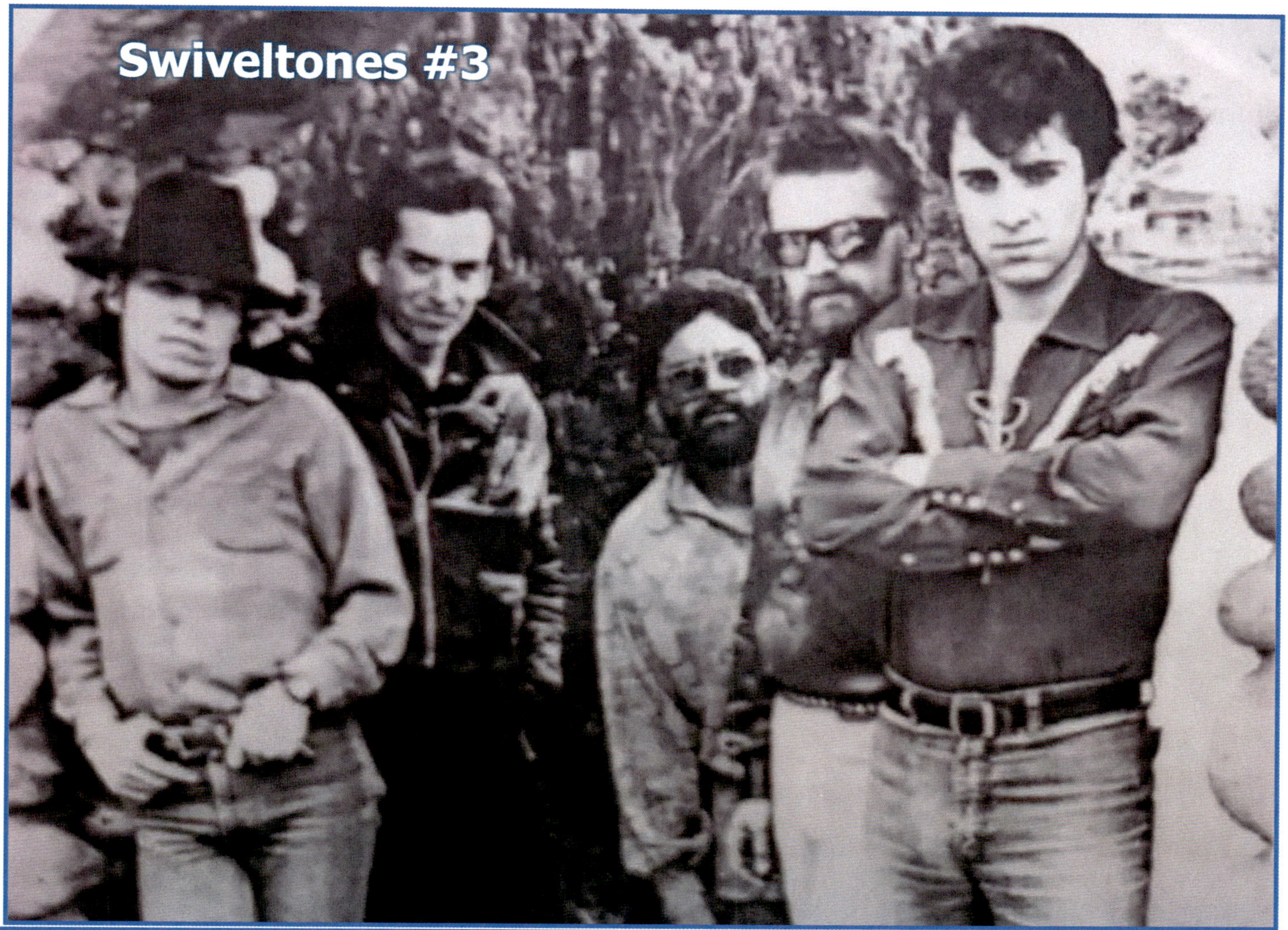

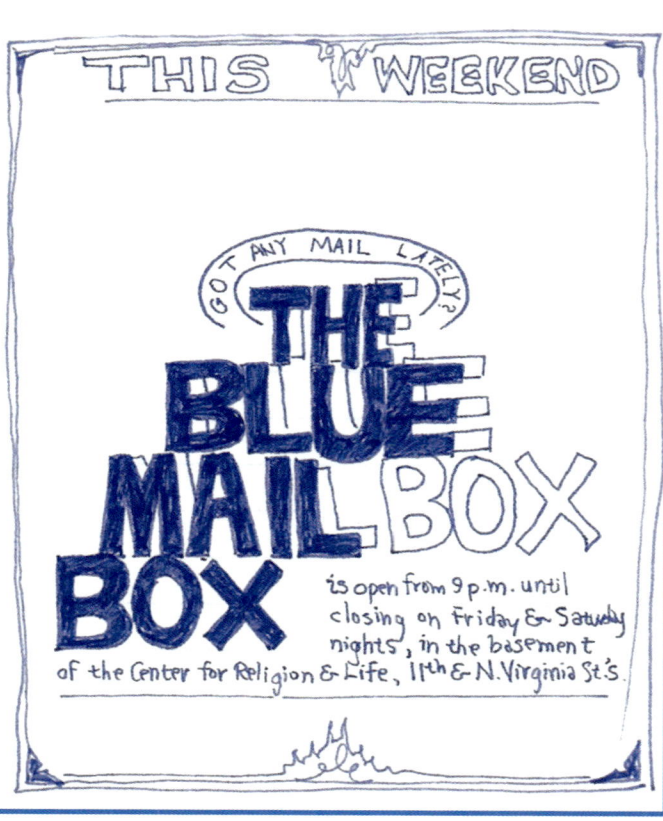

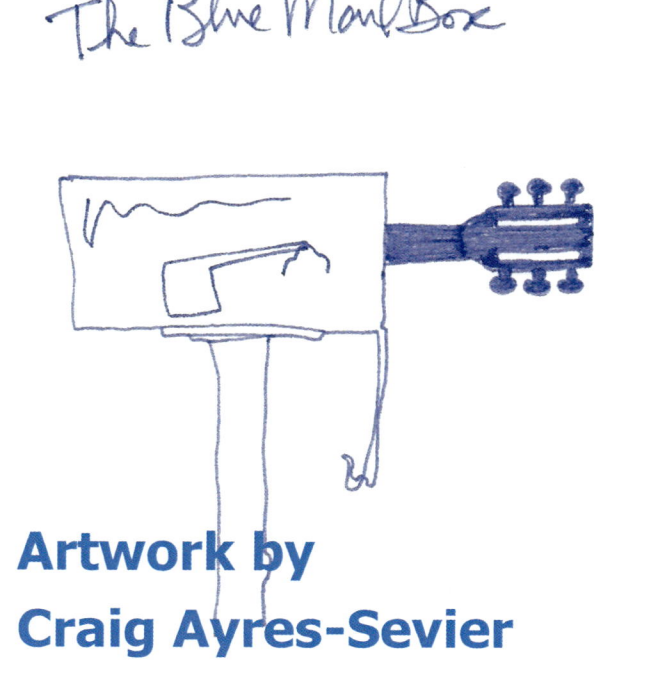

Artwork by Craig Ayres-Sevier

On occasion, our own Reno notables have rubbed shoulders with some of the biggest stars in the world of entertainment.

In these next few pages, we'd like to present some of those moments that were captured on film long before the advent of the cell phone!

Eddie

Alex

Sammy

Max

Rob Brooks

Max Volume with 3/4 of Van Halen

Greg Golden with Alice Cooper

Rob Hanna with Eddie Money

Kathy McCovey with Phil Kennemore and Leonard Haze—Y&T

Mike Mantor, Max Volume, and Robert Plant

Mike Reno (Loverboy), and Rob Hanna

Bruce Dickinson/ Kathy McCovey

Sandy Selby, Jay Leno, Gary Raffanelli, Johnny Ray

The Mamas & The Papas, left to right...Mike Mantor, MacKenzie Phillips, John Phillips, Denny Doherty, Steve Hobson, and Spanky McFarland down front

Greg Golden with Rudy Sarzo (Quiet Riot, Ozzy Osbourne, Whitesnake, and Dio)

Kathy McCovey with Ozzy Osbourne and 96 Rock staff members

Rob Hanna, Spike Orberg, Gayle , aka "Ziggy" Orberg (Spike's Mom) and Greg Allman

Mike Mantor and Kathy McCovey with Van Halen

Mike Mantor

Alex

Eddie

Sammy

Michael

Kathy McCovey

Greg Golden with Gunnar and Matthew Nelson

Mike Mantor with Dave Mason

Kathy McCovey with Clarence Clemons (Bruce Springsteen's E Street Band)

Mike Mantor with Jan & Dean

Mike Mantor with Craig Chaquico (Jefferson Starship)

Rob Hanna with Kenny Loggins

For MICHAEL
"WE STILL LOOK
GREAT"

Pat Travers
9/7/87

Mike Mantor with Pat Travers

Greg Golden with Eddie Money and Susan Cramer

Greg Golden with:

Upper Left: Jack Russell of Great White

Upper Right: Frank Hannon of Tesla

Lower Left: Jonathan Davis of Korn

Lower Right: Dave Mustaine of Metallica, and Megadeth, with Shanda Golden

203

Top Left: Mike Mantor with Paul Kantner (Jefferson Airplane, Jefferson Starship

Top Right: Mike Mantor with Roger Miller

Bottom: Jeff Mantor and Kathy McCovey with two-thirds of ZZ Top

Mike Mantor with Jeff Beck— 1976

Top left: Steve Hatley with the great Nicky Hopkins (Rolling Stones, Quicksilver Messenger Service, Jeff Beck and many others).

Top right: Paul Manktelow with Mr. Hopkins. Bottom left: Paul & Steve with Apollonia (Purple Rain). Bottom right: Paul with Spencer Davis

Glenn Bailey Becomes Max Volume

My parents moved to Reno in 1976. My stepmom had family here, and family vacations were always spent in the Reno area. We loved to camp in the area and explore the bounty of recreation it has to offer. I loved old Reno, going to family events in the Mapes Sky Room, the shows, the glamour and glitz of a cruise up Virginia Street with a pit stop at the Mayfair Market.

I had just graduated from high school in L.A. I had friends, a girlfriend, I played in a band. I used to go see Van Halen and Quiet Riot play backyard parties. I knew both bands. I almost had a deal as a solo singer-songwriter with a major label. Unfortunately, my father's health was not so good. My stepmom pleaded with me to move up to Reno and make peace with him. He was now retired, having been the Chief Deputy Coroner of L. A. County, where the morgue was full of dead guitar players. He was NOT on board with my musical pursuits!

On October 31st 1978, I packed up as many things as I'd need, tossed them into my 1967 Mercury Cougar XR7 and blasted up 395 to Reno. My parents' home was off Keystone. I knew no one. I got a job delivering for Shoshone Coca-Cola. I made some friends.

One of them was Tim Manfredi. Tim worked at Eucalyptus Records. He used to tell me to go to jam night at CBS Dance Floor on Grove Street (once a big-time disco, now a live music venue). One night I packed up my Gibson SG and went down to CBS to jam.

I walked in with my guitar. Nobody said a thing. I walked over to the bar and saw two guys that looked like rock band guys. I said "what time does the jam start?" It was Chuck Ruff and John Sanchez. Chuck looked at me and said, "Who the fuck are you?" I looked him straight in the eye and said, "I'm a guy that wants to play." John Sanchez says to me "You know any AC/DC?"

This was the beginning of a very long amazing friendship. I still miss Chuck. I don't see John much, but there's a bond that will always be. At that point the adventure began. I got a job at CBS Dance Floor as the DJ, light man, sound man, and sometimes opening act. I met everyone who was anyone in Reno. At some point I was sent to KOZZ to voice and produce the club's radio commercials. I met Bruce Van Dyke and Daniel Cook. We hit it off. We shared a lot of musical tastes.

When my father passed, I enrolled at UNR. My counselor recommended an internship at a radio station, KOZZ. I jumped on it. It was there that I was hired by Daniel Cook to be a DJ. By now I had also become a member of local rock band Terraplane. Jonnie G and I are still best friends.

From there, it exploded. I used to use a lot of silly names on the air: Stan Durd, Otto Matic, Phil Harmonic, Paul Molive, Jeff Leppard, and Hugh Betcha. When Kathy McCovey took a job at the top rock station in Fresno, Bruce told me to apply for the full-time overnight DJ slot. I said "but I'm the guy that does everything wrong." Bruce looked at me and said "in this business we call that talent."

I got the job. I met the owner of the company (Howard Kalmenson). He told me that I was hired because I was in college, and that was something I didn't have to do. He said "if you're going to work for me, I want someone who does things they don't have to do." 42 years later Howard and I are still enjoying the fruits of our labors.

Bruce congratulated me and said, "now get in there, start some shit and light up the phones." Daniel Cook sat me down in his office and went over some ground rules. Then he said "pick a name and stick with it. We're going into the ratings and you have to have one name." I said, "I'm going to be Max Volume."

I was never really a DJ. I was a fan with a microphone. You should be careful what you wish for. Becoming famous in your twenties reads like a page from the "Big Book of Bad Ideas." I made it work. Through the peaks and valleys, the feasts and the famines, it's always you that makes you you. Be you. Full blast you!

With Kathy McCovey - KOZZ

With Randy Webb and "Bud Girls"

Max

Max Volume and Mayor Pete Sferrazza present the key to the city to ZZ Top...Billy Gibbons, Frank Beard, and Dusty Hill

Daniel Cook, David Coverdale, Jimmy Page, Max Volume

Joe Perry (Aerosmith), and Max Volume

John Bon Jovi being interviewed by Max Volume

Max Volume, "The FIXX", Daniel Cook, and Harry Reynolds

Max Volume with Steven Tyler and Brad Whitford (Aerosmith)

Max with Kate Pierson "The B-52's"

We'd like to pause for a moment to pay tribute to some of our outstanding Reno disc jockeys, without whom the airwaves would be silent, not to mention boring. Here's a brief toast to some of our finest pur-veyors of music, banter, and round-the-clock fun and entertainment...

Bruce Van Dyke and Max Volume

Billy "The Janitor" Alverson, Daniel "The Sarge" Cook, and Max Volume

Mike Chase

Bob Schlesinger

Kathy McCovey (# 44)

KOZZ Staff, Left to right: Jody Detri, Lynette Bianchi (Doege), Steve Funk, and Billy "The Janitor" Alverson

Christiane Larsen Brown
KRZQ 96 Rock

Christine Clark, aka "Nicky Delaney", house DJ at Paul Revere's "Kicks", 90's

Steve Funk

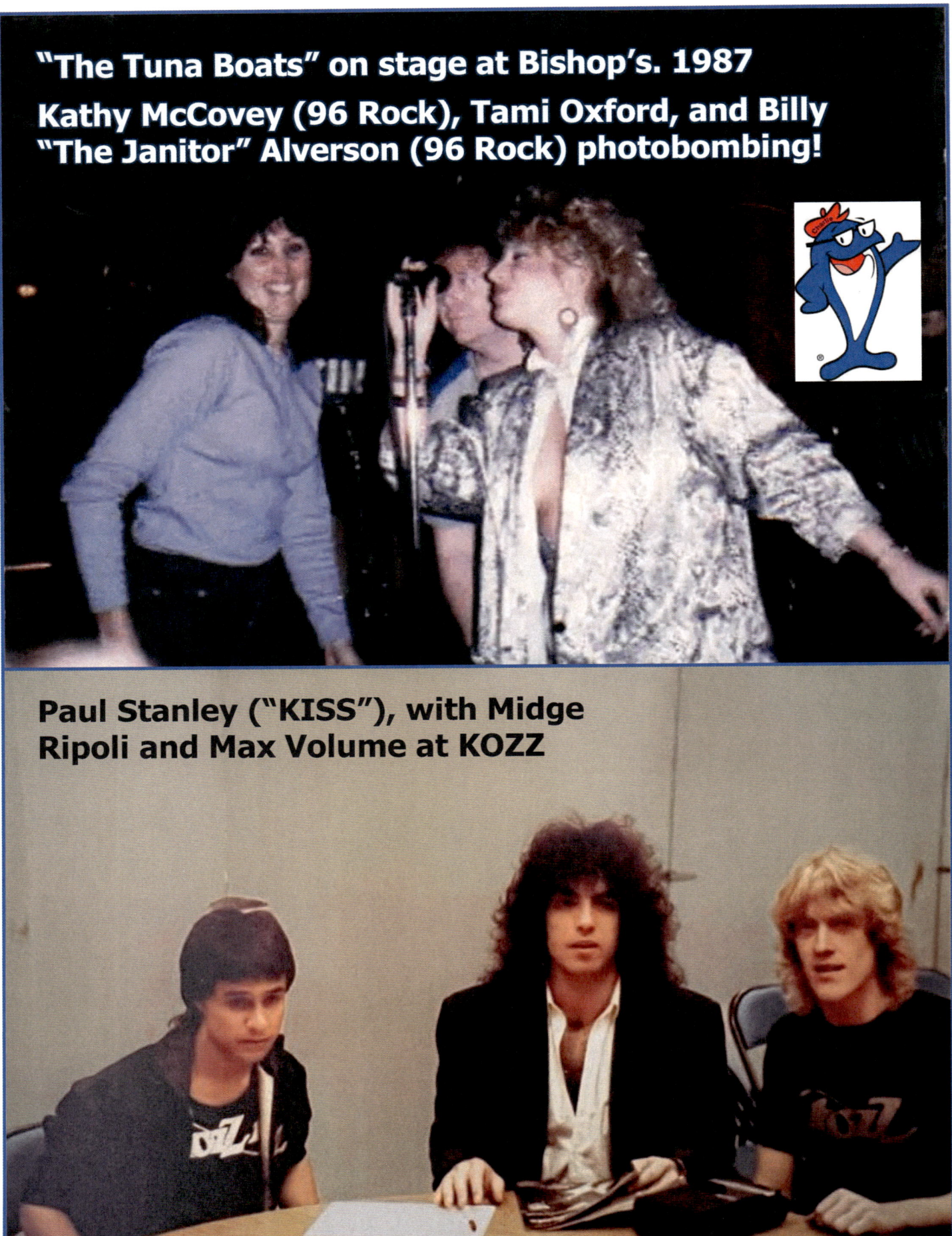

"The Tuna Boats" on stage at Bishop's. 1987
Kathy McCovey (96 Rock), Tami Oxford, and Billy "The Janitor" Alverson (96 Rock) photobombing!

Paul Stanley ("KISS"), with Midge Ripoli and Max Volume at KOZZ

218

Best of Luck, and eat my shorts..... All the best — [signature]

One of Reno's all-time great air personalities, Mr. Bruce Van Dyke. He introduced us to some of the finest music in our history over many decades. Rest in peace, BVD. You done good!

Jonnie G

"Terraplane"
1982

Rick Taylor
"Foolish Behaviour"
1983

the Grand Ballroom
presents

PAT TRAVERS

special guests
Stage Door Johnny
Mon. Sept. 7 8pm
ticket info:
827-4888

1987

My Name is Zella

Zella Lehr

HELEN LONG
and
THE LONG SHOTS

**Helen Long and
The Long Shots
1974**

The Zella Lehr Show

Skip Gillette

THE JERRY SUN SHOW

225

Kay Martin
and her
Bodyguards

THE ESQUIRES, a tradition on the Nevada lounge circuit, have returned to the Topaz Room of Nevada Lodge on the North Shore of Lake Tahoe. Their engagement runs through Feb. 28.

2 Popular Acts At Nevada Lodge

It's a battle of long-time favorites this week at North Lake Tahoe's lively Nevada Lodge where the Esquires and the Commodores share the spectacular Topaz Room spotlight.

The Esquires opened at Nevada Lodge Wednesday night (Feb. 15) to be greeted by a large number of fans who have attended every Esquire engagement at Nevada Lodge, going back over the years. The Esquires' vocal and instrumental talents have made them one of the top acts on the Reno-Tahoe-Las Vegas circuit; their background also includes movies, television and club dates throughout the nation.

SINGER'S DOUBLE LIFE

NEW YORK — George Roy, production singer at the Copacabana nightclub, doesn't get too much sleep. During the day he is personnel manager at a New Jersey typewriter plant. He is at the cafe until very late at night and in his business office at 8:30 a.m.

The Esquires' distinctive recording of "My Adobe Hacienda" is perhaps their best-known contribution to a galaxy of hit records. Nevada Lodge audiences applaud the Esquires' polished sense of music and comedy timing, and the virtuosity on piano, accordion and bass, shown by Bob Hanna, Joe Martini and Eddie Bee, respectively.

Musical fare ranges from soft and lyrical to big and bold, from old to new — always spiced by sight and sound gags that make the Esquires one of the freshest groups around. They are booked into Nevada Lodge through Feb. 28.

As a super treat for Nevada Lodge audiences, the Commodores are also appearing on the Topaz Room stage, alternating with the Esquires. The Commodores are renowned as vocalists and for their ability to put across amazing impressions of other singers — both singles and groups. They are scheduled to appear at Nevada Lodge through Feb. 27.

Hall and January

MUSIC AND ART FESTIVAL

Elvin Bishop
Norton Buffalo
Wade Brothers Band
Johnny Lundemo & the Shades

Nevada Day, October 31, 1985
T-Car Speedway Carson City

Gates open at 12:30 p.m.
Show starts at 1:30 p.m.

Budget Tapes & Records
Mirabelli's
Deadhead
Clementine's
Jobe's

Buy now — limited seating

Children Under 13 Free

$12.50 Advance   **$14.00 Gate**

Jerry Kratzmeyer—1976

HOMEMADE JAM

Bangalore Choir

229

Russ Miller & Steve Funk

Steve Funk

A Brief History! The Smoking Caterpillars were founded in 1995 by Bill Blackley and Tim Holst. Although there were many personnel changes, the main players were guitarist/vocals Bill Blackley, keyboardist/vocals Tim Holst, guitarist Mark Frybarger, vocalist Greg Darnell, bassist/vocals Ned Chaney and drummer/vocals Rick Strobel. KOZZ DJ Max Volume was an honorary member of the band who would join us on stage on several occasions. The band played all over Northern Nevada and Northern California playing mostly bars, festivals and major shows, opening for such acts as Kansas, BTO, and Reo Speedwagon. Their song "Flying" was selected as the first song on KOZZ's Home Grown cd. They produced two cd's of original music written by Blackley, Holst and Darnell.

Bill Blackley

The Smoking Caterpillars

SAT. FEB. 27 SMOKING CATERPILLARS RED DOG SALOON Virginia City, Nevada ☎ (775) 847-7700

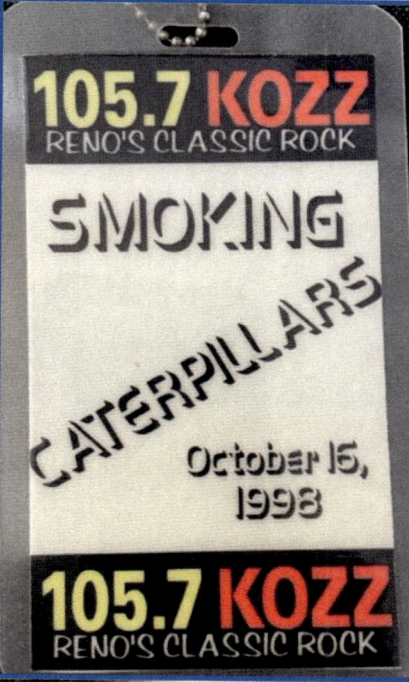

105.7 KOZZ RENO'S CLASSIC ROCK SMOKING CATERPILLARS October 15, 1998 105.7 KOZZ RENO'S CLASSIC ROCK

105.7 KOZZ RENO'S CLASSIC ROCK First Annual Free Concert Presenting: October 16, 1998 Lawlor Events Center 7:00 pm KANSAS & With Special Guest SMOKEN' CATEPILLARS Listen to 105.7 KOZZ

105.7 KOZZ RENO'S CLASSIC ROCK PRESENTS Nº 7489 Kansas & America WITH THE SMOKING CATEPILLARS FRIDAY, OCTOBER 16, 1998 7:00 PM LAWLOR EVENTS CENTER $30.00 VALUE General Admission. Does not Guarantee Admission.

105.7 KOZZ RENO'S CLASSIC ROCK Atlantis Coors Light Coors Present Summer Fest 2000 Featuring AMERICA BTO Jefferson Starship The Fabulous Thunderbirds Plus! The Jamie Rollins Band & The Smoking Caterpillars FREE Listener Appreciation Concert Atlantis Casino Resort Parking Venue on South Virginia Street July 15, 00 • Doors Open at Noon to 9:00PM Listen to 105.7 KOZZ for ticket locations.

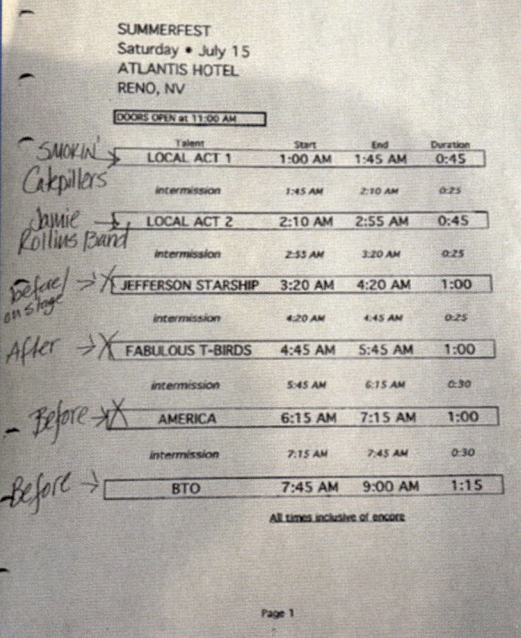

SUMMERFEST Saturday • July 15 ATLANTIS HOTEL RENO, NV

DOORS OPEN at 11:00 AM

	Talent	Start	End	Duration
Smokin' Catepillars	LOCAL ACT 1	1:00 AM	1:45 AM	0:45
	intermission	1:45 AM	2:10 AM	0:25
Jamie Rollins Band	LOCAL ACT 2	2:10 AM	2:55 AM	0:45
	intermission	2:55 AM	3:20 AM	0:25
Before on stage	JEFFERSON STARSHIP	3:20 AM	4:20 AM	1:00
	intermission	4:20 AM	4:45 AM	0:25
After	FABULOUS T-BIRDS	4:45 AM	5:45 AM	1:00
	intermission	5:45 AM	6:15 AM	0:30
Before	AMERICA	6:15 AM	7:15 AM	1:00
	intermission	7:15 AM	7:45 AM	0:30
Before	BTO	7:45 AM	9:00 AM	1:15

All times inclusive of encore

Page 1

T-Car Speedway Presents in Carson City
the
SPRING ROCK FESTIVAL
featuring

Bo Diddley
with
Lady Bo and the Family Jewel
Country Joe McDonald
Stone Ground

Cold Blood
with
Lydia Dense
Booker T
Sutro Symphony Orchestra

Plus Special Guest Stars
David LaFlamme, Hal Waggenet, Mitchel Holmes & Friends
reformed original members of

"It's A Beautful Day"
Sunday, May 25
T-Car Speedway

Intersection of Hyway 50 and Hyway 395 between Reno and Southshore Lake Tahoe
ADULT BEVERAGES SOLD • ARTS AND CRAFTS DISPLAYS • 9 HOURS OF MUSIC
GATES OPEN 10 A.M. • $5 IN ADVANCE • $6 AT THE GATE • SHOW STARTS 12 NOON

CARSON CITY: T-Car Speedway, C-J Burger Factory, Jim Boy's Tacos. RENO:
Discount Records, Nevada Auto Sound, Korky's (parklane center)
Eucalyptus Records. SPARKS: Record Corrall. SOUTH LAKE TAHOE: Back
O'Beyond, Dead Head Record INCLINE: Grog & Grist.

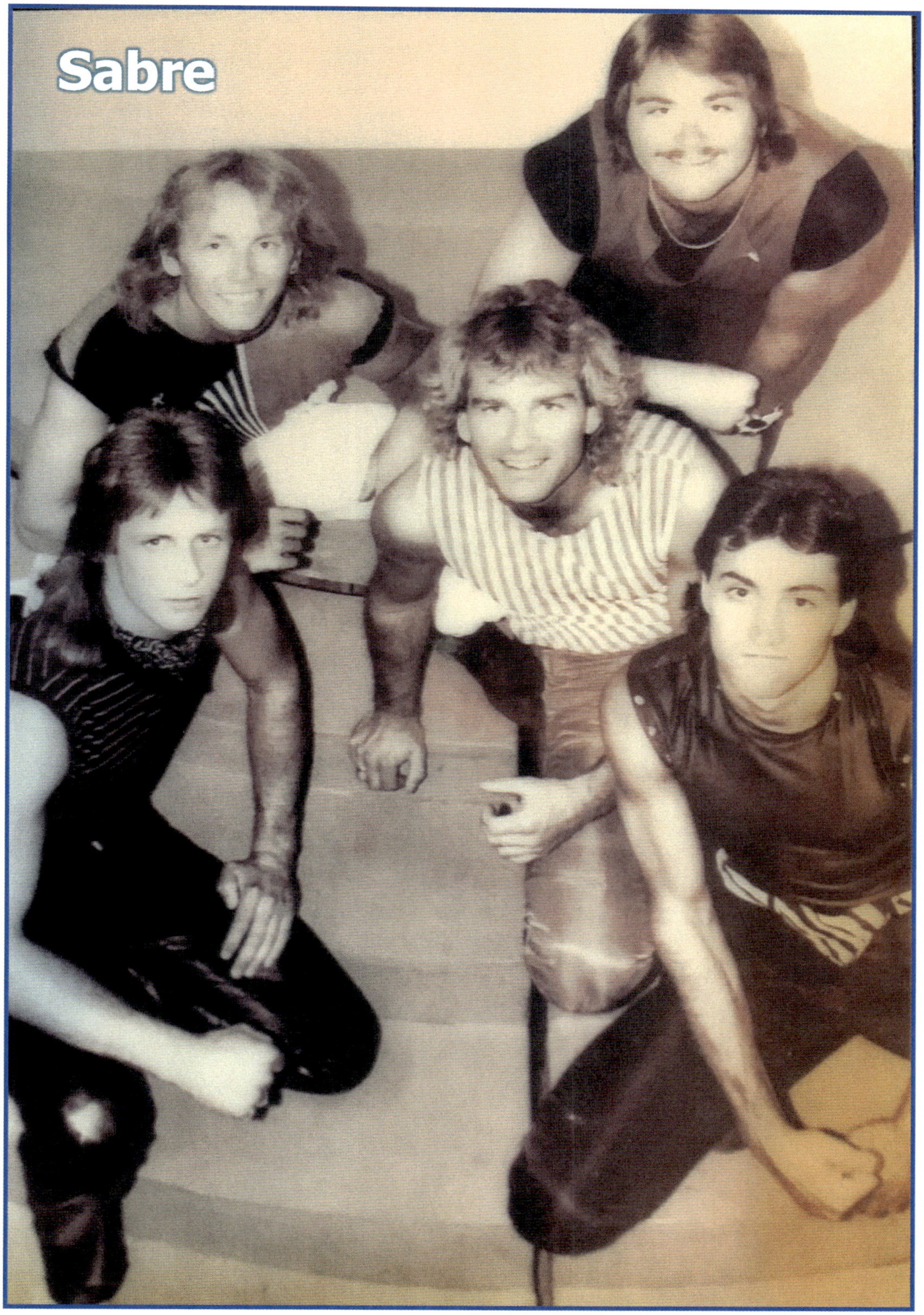
Sabre

NEW YEARS EVE PARTY
featuring
SABRE
— 9 p.m. – 2 a.m. —
SUSANVILLE
MEMORIAL HALL
Tickets are Limited
Including 2 Bars
Admission $4.00 — at the door $5.50
PLEASE — NO ONE UNDER 18 YRS.

No. 237
HALLOWEEN PARTY
OCTOBER 27th / 8:00 P.M.
at
MEMORIAL HALL
ADMISSION $3.50
COSTUME REQUIRED
OCT. 27th
8:00 PM
MEMORIAL HALL
PROCEEDS TO :
MUSIC BY:
Sabre
PLEASE - NO ONE UNDER 18 yrs.
No. 237

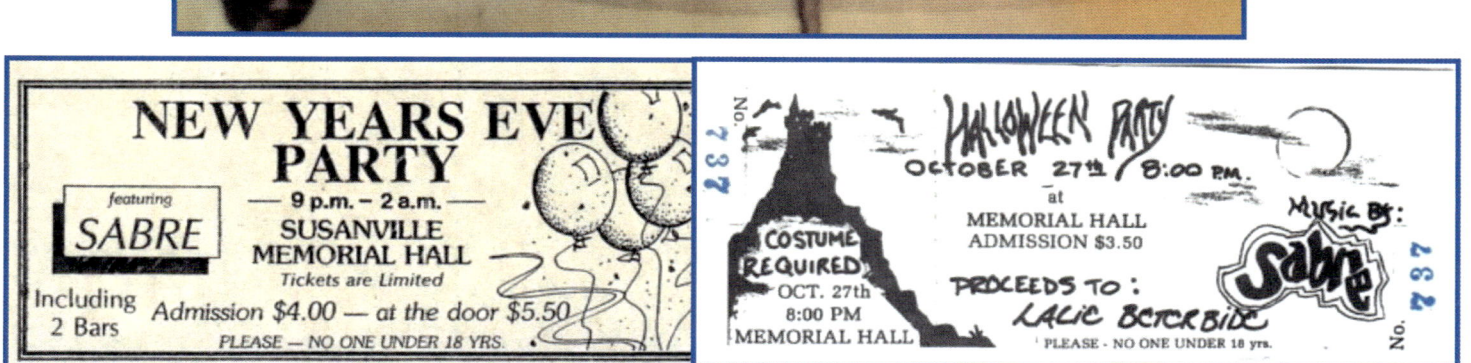

Ron Barron

Rayge Reunion—1998

Rob Hanna with Foolish Behaviour & friends in Guadalajara, Mexico...Ole!

Greg Golden

Model: Shanda Golden

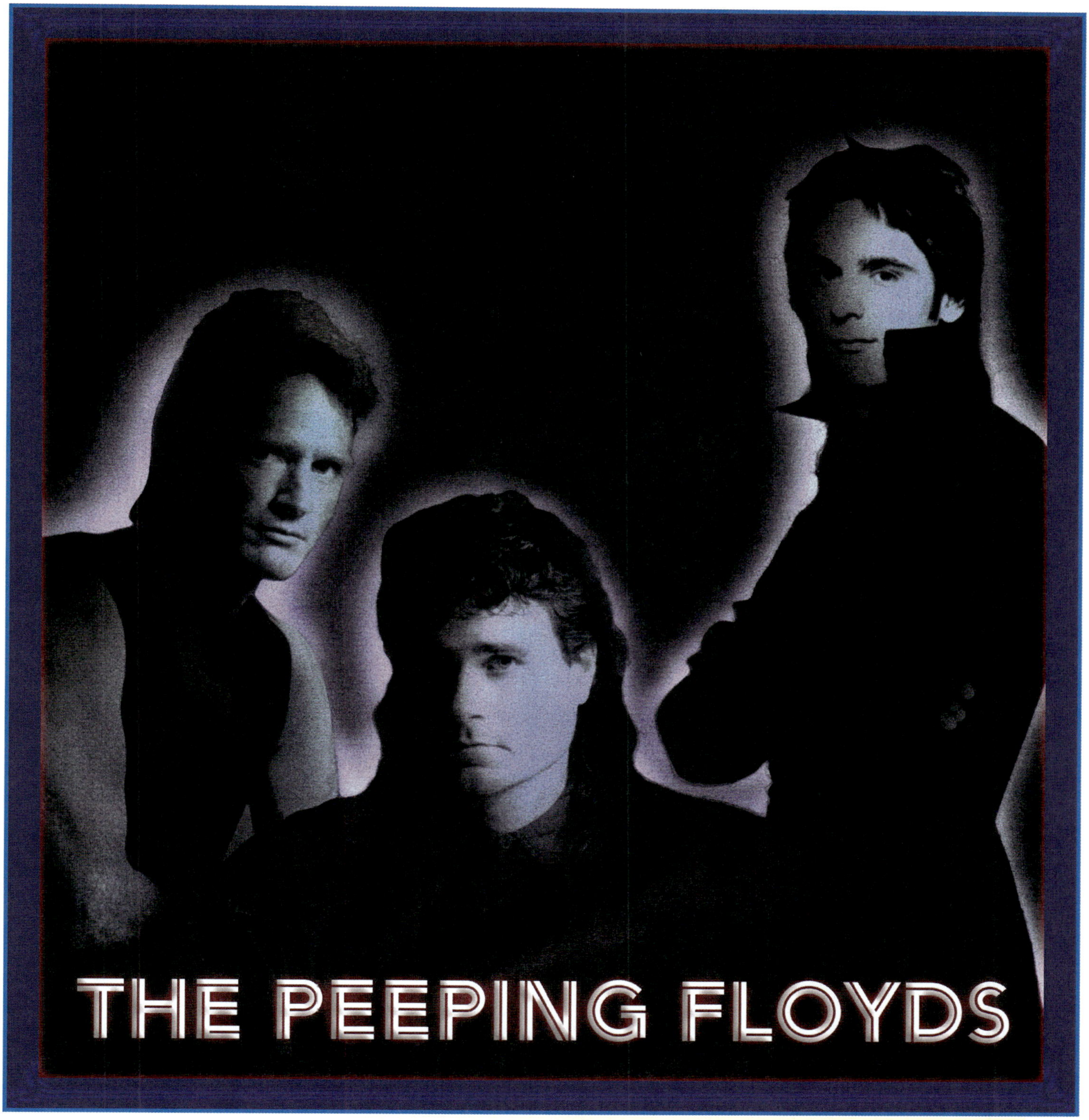

THE PEEPING FLOYDS

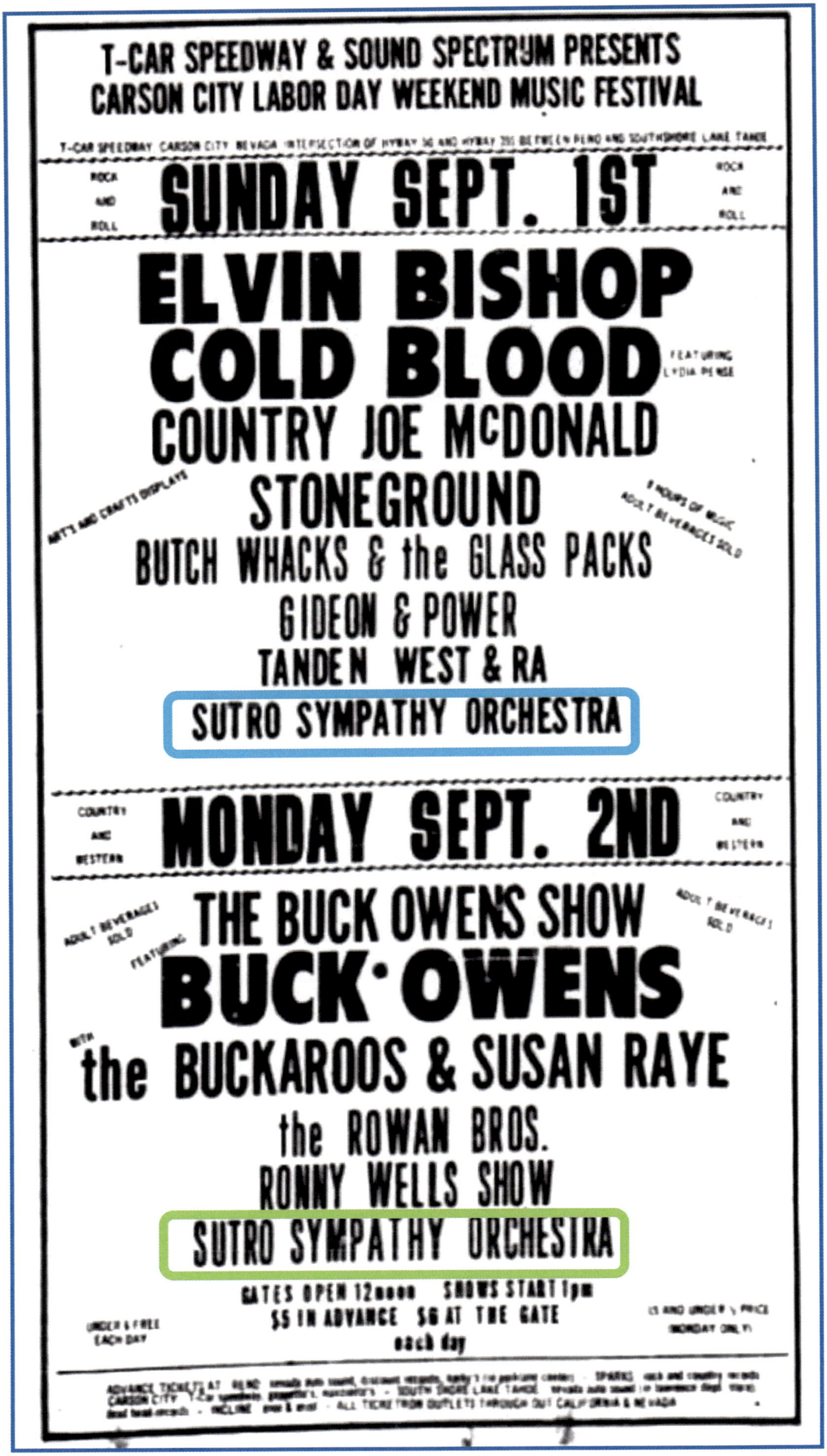

T-CAR SPEEDWAY & SOUND SPECTRUM PRESENTS
CARSON CITY LABOR DAY WEEKEND MUSIC FESTIVAL

T-CAR SPEEDWAY CARSON CITY NEVADA INTERSECTION OF HYWAY 36 AND HYWAY 395 BETWEEN RENO AND SOUTHSHORE LAKE TAHOE

ROCK AND ROLL

SUNDAY SEPT. 1ST

ROCK AND ROLL

ELVIN BISHOP
COLD BLOOD
FEATURING LYDIA PENSE

COUNTRY JOE McDONALD
STONEGROUND

ART'S AND CRAFTS DISPLAYS

9 HOURS OF MUSIC
ADULT BEVERAGES SOLD

BUTCH WHACKS & the GLASS PACKS
GIDEON & POWER
TANDEN WEST & RA
SUTRO SYMPATHY ORCHESTRA

COUNTRY AND WESTERN

MONDAY SEPT. 2ND

COUNTRY AND WESTERN

ADULT BEVERAGES SOLD

ADULT BEVERAGES SOLD

THE BUCK OWENS SHOW
FEATURING
BUCK·OWENS
WITH
the BUCKAROOS & SUSAN RAYE
the ROWAN BROS.
RONNY WELLS SHOW
SUTRO SYMPATHY ORCHESTRA

GATES OPEN 12 noon   SHOWS START 1pm
$5 IN ADVANCE $6 AT THE GATE
each day

UNDER 6 FREE
EACH DAY

15 AND UNDER ½ PRICE
MONDAY ONLY)

ADVANCE TICKETS AT   RENO nevada auto sound, discount records, harry's the perfume center   SPARKS rock and country records
CARSON CITY T-Car speedway grapevine's macdonald's   SOUTH SHORE LAKE TAHOE nevada auto sound (ex lawrence floyd store)
dead head records   INCLINE ernie & earl   ALL TICKETRON OUTLETS THROUGH OUT CALIFORNIA & NEVADA

**Jerry & Billy Kratzmeyer
1971**

**Boxer—Guam
1982**

11th Annual   Contribute to a Great Cause

SWEETHOP 98

Celebrate With Your Sweetheart!

Saturday, February 14th at 8:00 pm
The Reno Hilton

$15.00* per person • Must be 21 or over

Advance ticket sales at all Raley's camera departments
*Ticket price includes one $5.00 chance for raffle drawing.

DANCE TO ROCK 'N ROLL HITS OF THE 50'S, 60'S & 70'S

featuring

Papa Clutch & the Shifters

All proceeds will be donated to
*Food For Families in cooperation
with the Salvation Army and the
Food Bank of Northern Nevada*

SPONSORS:

  RenoAir
Discover A Better Low Fare Airline

Corporate and reserved tables are available. Please call the information line 747-1628.

Papa Clutch and The Shifters

243

PAPA CLUTCH AND THE SHIFTERS

FROG ROCK

1967

1955—2014

STEVEN

JAMES

HOBSON

Skip Gillette-'World War III" —Whisky A Go Go, L.A.

Skip Gillette

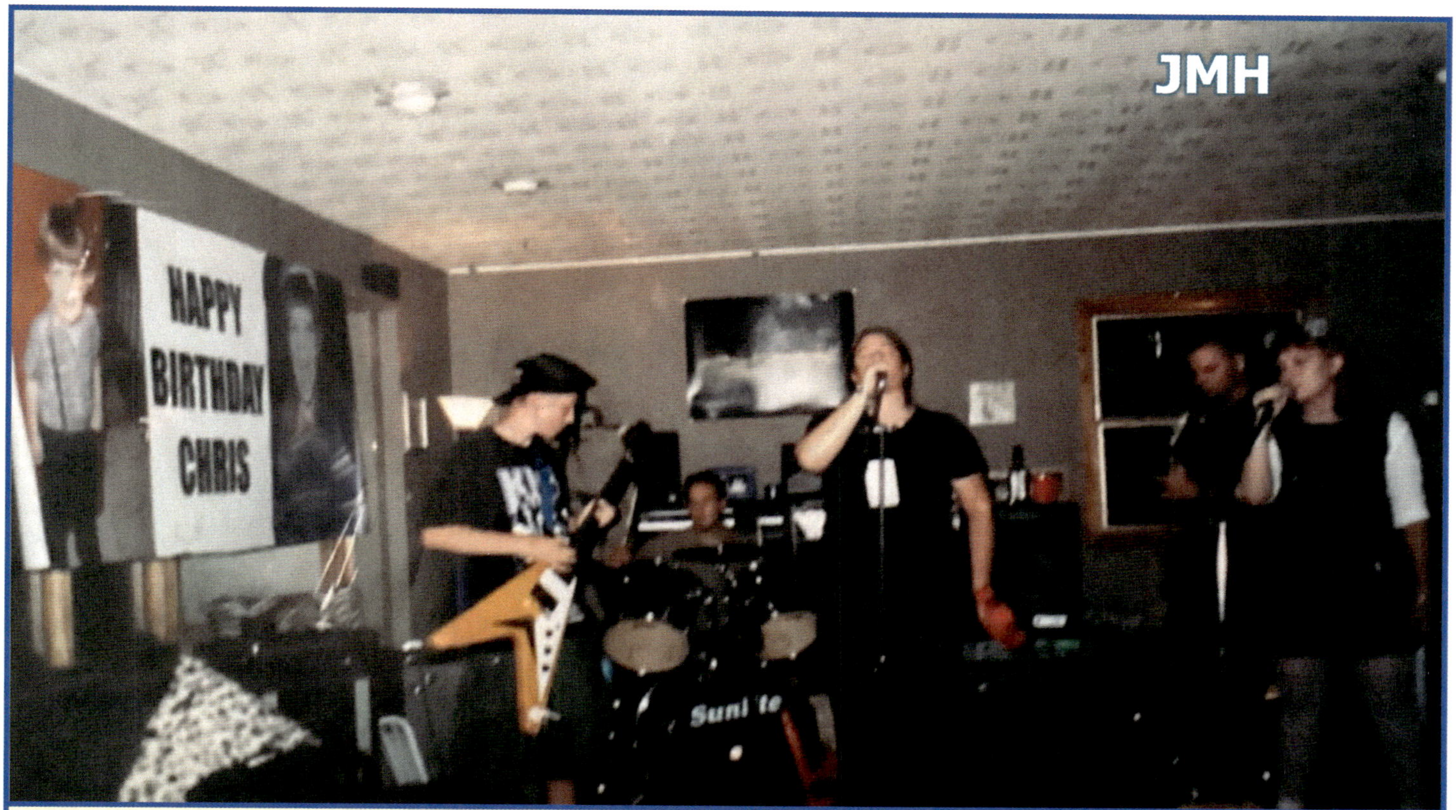
JMH
HAPPY
BIRTHDAY
CHRIS

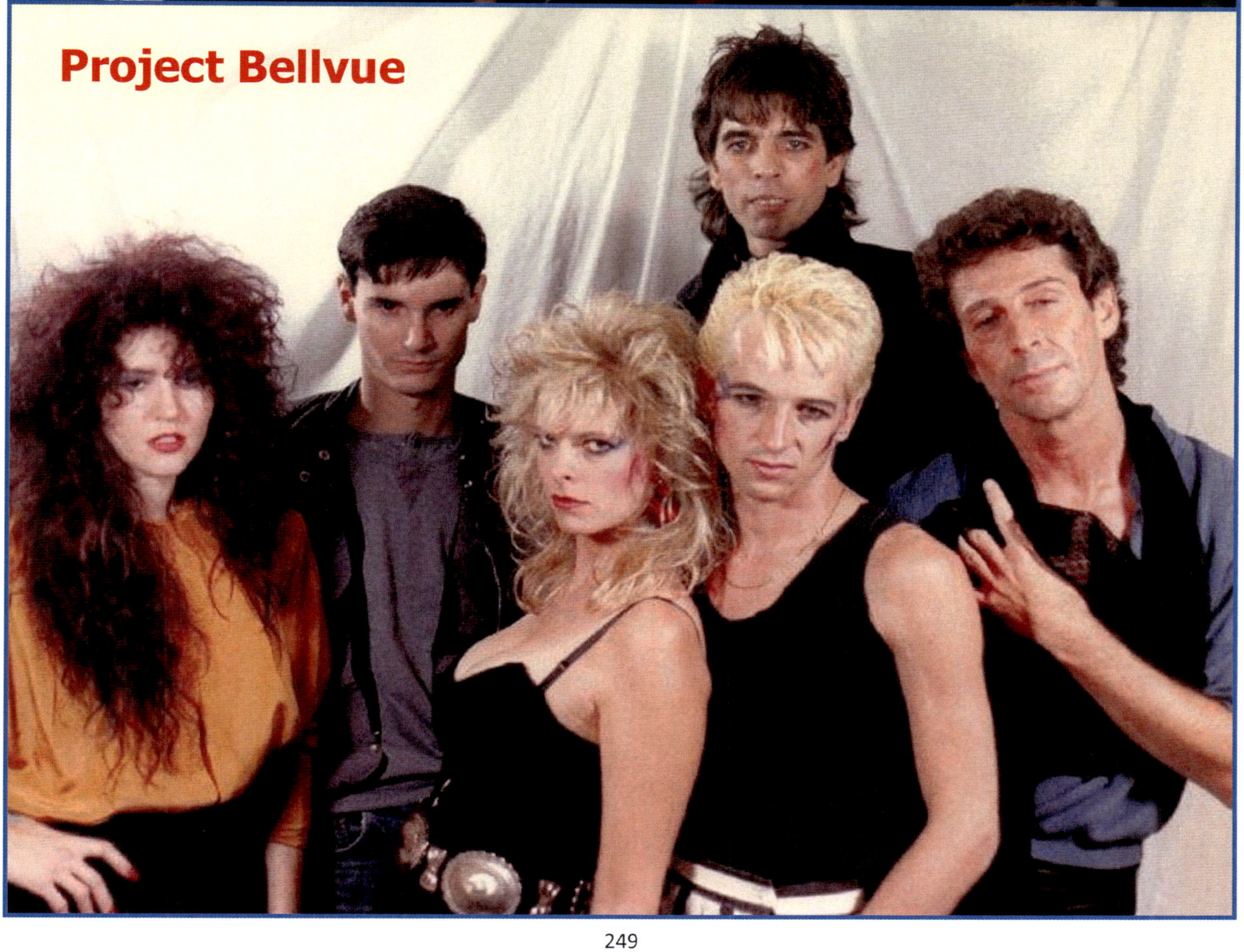
Project Bellvue

Broken Promise

POWER HOUSE

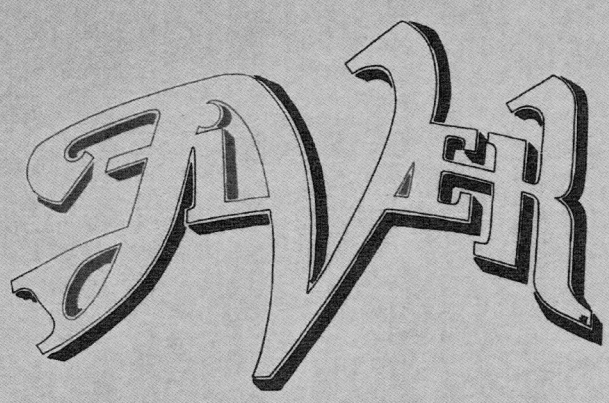

Since their first engagement in January of 1976 when they opened a "Foghat" concert in Medford, Oregon, "FIVER" has rapidly become one of the most sought-after rock and roll attractions in the western United States. In the seven months since that first appearance, "FIVER" has appeared in twenty-two of the better-known rock clubs and taverns in the Northwest, as well as several concert appearances with major acts.

"FIVER" carries with them on the road the finest available sound equipment, capable of covering an audience up to 5,000 people, as well as a complete lighting system, fogger, and other stage and visual effects.

Listed below is the upcoming itinerary for "FIVER" for the remainder of 1976. Several dates are still available for booking, so, if you're interested in the act, contact Head First Productions for further information, at (702) 323-0378, or write to us at 1280 Terminal Way, Suite 32, Reno, Nevada 89502.

Thank you.

August 19 — 22	The K & D	Medford, Oregon
August 24 — 28	Captain Coyote's	Olympia, Washington
August 29 —	The Breakers	Pt. Roberts, Washington
August 30 — Sept. 1	(Open)	
September 2 — 4	Rocker Tavern	Aberdeen, Washington
September 5	My Place Tavern	Seattle, Washington
September 7 — 19	Poop Deck	Kent, Washington
September 21 — 25	Golden Drift	Nelson, B. C. (Canada)
September 29 — Oct. 2	El Patio	Stateline, Idaho
October 4 — 9	Off, Vacation	
October 11 — 23	The Silver Cloud	Salt Lake City, Utah
October 25 — 31	The Triangle	Albuquerque, New Mexico
November 2 — 7	Choo Choo's	Tucson, Arizona
November 8 — 13	Off, Vacation	
NOvember 15 — 21	(Open)	
November 23 — 27	Eagers Place	Everett, Washington
November 28	The Breakers	Pt. Roberts, Washington
November 30 — Dec. 12	The Attic	Longview, Washington
December 13 — 18	(Open)	
December 20 — 26	Off, Vacation	
December 27 — Jan. 2	(Open)	

lookout...
by DENNY JONES

This was pretty much a weekend of R and R, rest and recuperation, but I did manage to get out for a little hard rock and carousing Saturday night.

This was after I had attended a fantastic crab and steak bar-b-que at the Air Guard where I got to rub elbows with such famous local media types as **Marilyn Newton**, while listening to the strains of a local country group known as BO and the **SODOMIZERS**. Perhaps you'd better check for accuracy on that one as I got the name via a slightly inebriated Air Guard member. You know how things are in the wee, wee hours...

Anyway, after we'd stuffed ourselves with crab and steak and seven-sevens, it was over to the Elegant Wagon for a touch of the heavy metal sound. **Steve Layman** greeted us rather greedily and monetarily at the door with the excuse that since A' La Mode was playing, we'd have to pay a cover charge. Hey, okay by me. I've been paying covers for A' La Mode for about as long as I can remember. I probably own half-interest in their P.A. system by now.

Whatever. Layman was right there to make sure that he got his two bucks. When questioned on the future existence of hard rock at the Elegant Wagon, he informed me that he was switching over to disco in a week or so. When I expressed my somewhat muted dismay, he hastened to add that they would still feature live music occasionally, maybe once a month or so. But only really good groups, he emphasized...

Well, I've always considered A' La Mode a pretty good group. Their sound was a little indistinct, however. But by the time that I arrived I was already a few drinks along and I'm sure that everyone else was too. The Elegant Wagon was packed with appreciative souls and the boys in the band put on a quite a show. They're all excellent musical technicians.

Steve Hatley is still the keyboard genius that I've known for years, doubling on guitar and bass while **Jerry Weims** switched back and forth from bass to lead. Now, you know this has got to be something good when Jerry, who did a good solid stint as Edgar Winter's lead guitar player a few years back, is now handling the bass chores. Talk about a heavy lead back-up.

Jerry Weims, in my opinion, is the one to watch in this group. He has a real sense of originality in his music. Rather than just being a superb technician, he is also an extremely innovative and competent musician. He is one of the most talented

products of the local rock and roll culture...

Rob Hanna, an immensely expressive vocalist, also performed a few Rod Stewart impression tunes. Hanna will be featured this weekend with his TRIBUTE TO ROD STEWART set. If the other night was any indication, the show would be well worth catching.

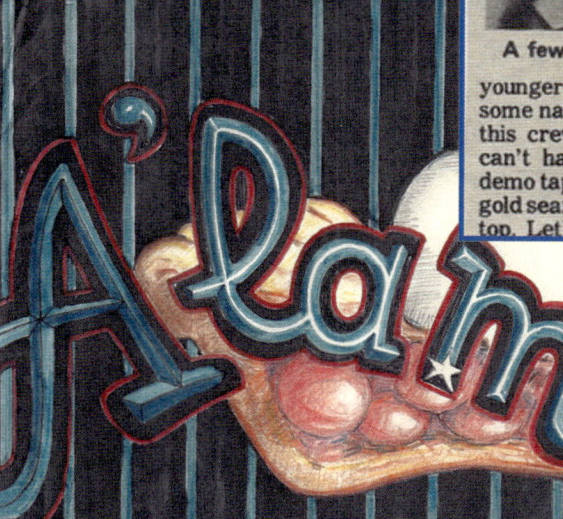

One of the reasons that I end up with the Sunday morning wobblies is that I patronize such establishments as the **OUT OF SIGHT** club, 4755 North Virginia, on Saturday night. Rock and roll has found an alternative to the Townhouse and I'm happy to say that it's live and doing well out on north 395. The Out of Sight club has been called more names that I've got fingers and that's not just by people who have been thrown out. This club has gone through a lot of changes. Rock, country, back to rock, just a bar where you can play pool, back to rock, maybe even disco; this place has been around the block more than just a few times. More bankruptcies have been filed than a deck has cards. But, and I really don't know why folks, the old place looks healthy and I think it's going to make it this time around. **A' LA MODE** played there Wednesday through Saturday last week. **SUTRO** has been a regular band at this non-descript club...

A' La Mode has reached that stage, or rather, the members of A' La Mode have reached that stage where they're going for that big recording contract. No more bouncing up and down the West Coast, playing every little rock and roll club up and down Interstate 5. These guys have been playing rock music ever since I've been in the area and it's quickly becoming a make it or break it situation. They're not getting any

A few of A' La Mode

younger and neither am I. I want to see some nationally known stars come out of this crew and there's no reason why it can't happen. The talent is there. The demo tapes are ready. It's time to hit that gold seam that will take them right to the top. Let's go...

THE ACT

Richard (the artist formerly known as "Dick") Washburn

MADISON AVENUE

Max Danger

702

Steve Hatley

Chuck Ruff Group

THE LOCAL 205

Blind Date

Hardly Small

258

Chuck Ruff Group with
Red Dawn

The Kidds

STEVE DUNWOODIE (1950-2011)

April 22, 1950 - January 1, 2011)

Fans of Santa Barbara's **Big Brother Ernie Joseph** are saddened to hear the news of the passing of the band's drummer, **Steve ("Stevie D") Dunwoodie**. Steve passed away at Renown Medical Center, in Reno, Nevada, on New Years Day, 2011.

Steve was a kindhearted and loving father who also had more than just a knack for playing drums. To everyone who knew him, he was the best in the business.

After touring the southern United States in 1969 and 70 with Big Brother Ernie Joseph, Steve eventually decided to settle down with a wife and family while pursuing a career in warehousing. Earlier, Steve performed with **Jonathan Goodlife**, and the **Grateful Dead**.

Ernie Joseph remembers Steve as a charismatic, tireless performer who left the audience screaming. *"Steve's energy pumped up the whole band to do better, beyond our capability."*

Known for his vibrant solos during which he played with his sticks on fire, Steve set the energetic pace for all of Big Brother's shows.

"We first met Steve when his band, Jonathon Goodlife, did a show with us at Lake Tahoe, California. We were totally impressed with his drumming and showmanship. He joined us for the Southeast Tour with the Big Brother Ernie Joseph band. Steve was a superstar team player, really a stand-out drummer. Steve would take-off on the song ESP with a 20-minute drum solo, where he would play, then play with his hands, then walk off the drum set still playing with his sticks. Then he would tap on the mic and his body and "sing" drum parts. He would then get the crowd chanting repeatedly, "Peace now! Peace now!" He would finish his drum solo playing with his sticks on fire and, incredibly, he made his magic happen consistently every performance. Like everytime he got the ball, like a superstar football player, he would take it all the way to score big time. Steve was amazing with his contagious non-stop positive energy and his drive and determination. We all did our part, but Steve's energy took us to another level. He really made us a complete concert act, and the crowds loved it!"

Bill "The Electric" Church

So Inclined

STROKES AND JOKES: Danny Marona.

The Mary Kaye Trio

CORK PROCTOR

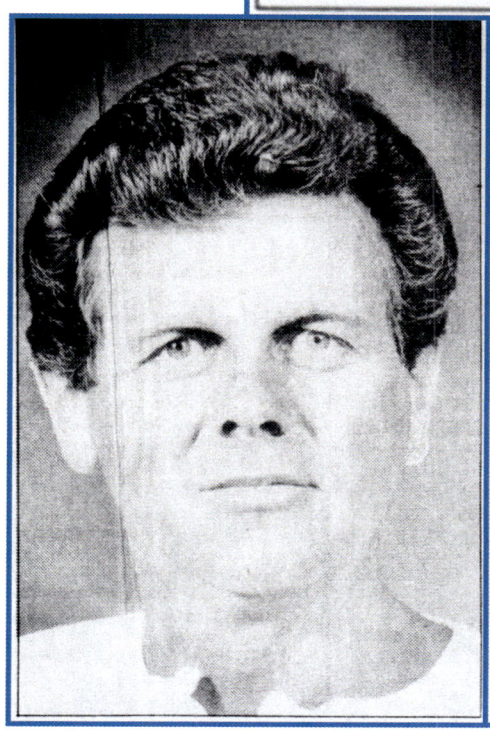

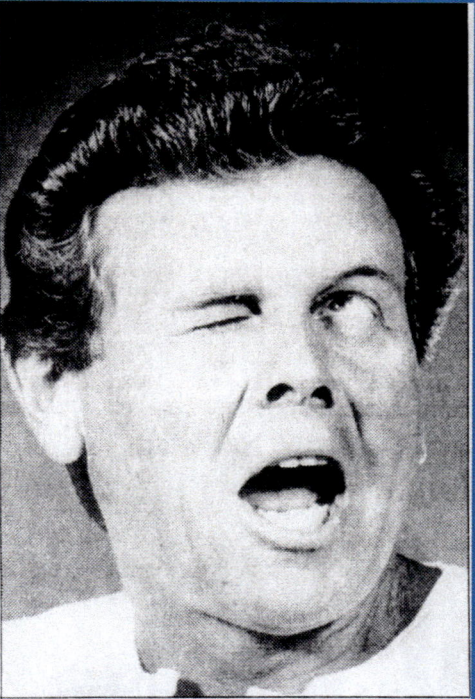

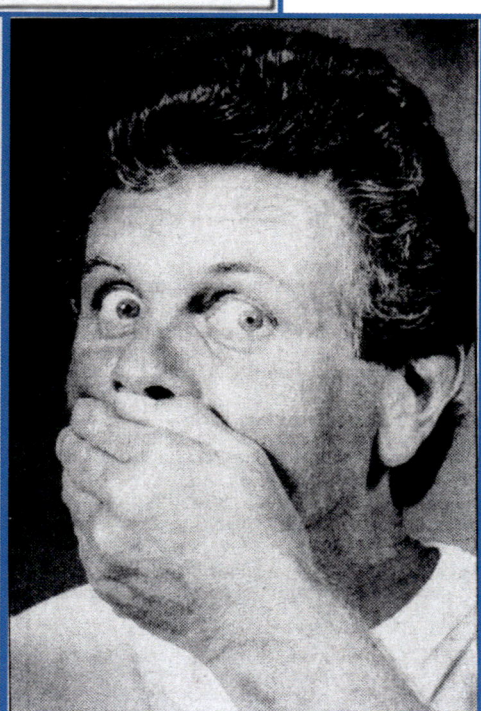

B.B. Morse

Reno Photographer, David Rocco, with...

Paul Revere

Klaus Meine and Rudy Schenker- "Scorpions"

Rob Halford-"Judas Priest"

"Loverboy"

Dave Mason

Wade Brothers Band

Gary Wade & The Bump

GARY WADE & THE BUMP

Nightfire

Lewd Vagrancy

267

WW III

Ménage à Trois

RICK PHILLIPS CAME TO L.A. IN 1978 AND JOINED FORCES WITH CHRYSALIS RECORDING ARTISTS "THE BABYS". RICK, COUPLED WITH TONY BROCK (CURRENTLY w/ ROD STEWART) NOW ADDED A DYNAMIC RHYTHM SECTION TO THE BAND. HE AND JONATHAN CAIN (w/ JOURNEY) JOINED TOGETHER AND CONTRIBUTED AS SINGER/SONG-WRITERS AS WELL AS PERFORMERS. RICK PENNED THE TITLE CUT OF HIS FIRST ALBUM WITH THE BAND, "UNION JACKS" SINCE THEN HE HAS BEEN ACTIVELY INVOLVED WITH VARIOUS STUDIO AND TOUR-ING PROJECTS.

SKIP GILLETTE HAS CREAT[ED] SOMEWHAT OF A FOLLOWING AMONG MUSICIANS, SPECIFI[CALLY] DRUMMERS, OVER THE PAST [?] YEARS FOR HIS UNIQUE ST[YLE] SOMETIMES TRIBAL, SOMETI[MES] WITH FUSION OVERTONES B[UT] ALWAYS RHYTHMIC, SKIP HA[S] CREATED A RECOGNIZABLE PRINT STYLE UNIQUELY HI[S] SKIP IS MOST NOTED FOR H[IS] WORK WITH "GAMMA" (A HAN[D?] PICKED BAND PUT TOGETHE[R] RONNIE MONTROSE). HIS [RE]CORDING AND EXTENSIVE T[OUR]ING EXPERIENCE ADDS TO [HIS] CONTRIBUTION MAKING HI[M] EXCITING TO WATCH AS TO[?].

CHRISSY SHEFTS, BEFORE MOVING FROM SEATTLE TO L.A., RECORDED AND TOURED WITH THE DIXON HOUSE BAND, OPENING SHOWS FOR HEART. NANCY WILSON (GUITARIST/HEART) ASKED CHRISSY TO PLAY ON HEART'S BEBE LE STRANGE ALBUM. THE RESULT, A POWERFUL DISPLAY OF CHRISSY'S WORK ON THE TITLE CUT. SHE HAS PERFORMED &/or RECORDED W/TIM BOGERT (JEFF BECK&VANILLA FUDGE) TONY BROCK & WALLY STOCKER (THE BABYS & ROD STEWART) AND MARK GOLDENBERG (WRITER/PERFORMER-LINDA RONSTADT/PETER FRAMPTON). CHRISSY'S EXTENSIVE MUSICAL TRAINING IS WELL SHOWCASED IN HER GUITAR AND SONGWRITING ARTISTRY.

Skip Gillette

LEE MARQUETTE & JOE SAVAGE

'Savage Experience' continues at Harrah's

Michele Lundeen
"The Queen of Steam"!

B.B. & The Boomers

272

273

BIFF ADAMS
Merle Haggard's Drummer

NORM ALDEN
*Famous for drowning in a bowl
of Mary Hartman's chicken soup*

LANCE ALWORTH
*Member Pro-football Hall of Fame
First AFL star to be Enshrined*

JUDY BAILEY
Country Singer

BRUCE BRESLOW
Mayor of Sparks Nevada

DON CHERRY
The Singer's Singer

KENNY "BOB" DAVIS
Country Comedian & Actor

MANCIL DAVIS
"Mr. Hole-in-one"

DAVID DOYLE
Actor

MERLE HAGGARD
Legendary "Poet of the Common Man"

DOUG KERSHAW
*Award winning fiddle player
"The Louisiana Man"*

SHELBY LYNNE
Country Singer

JIM MAC GEORGE
*Musical Comedian
Stan Laurel Impersonator Extraordinaire*

JOE AND ABE MANUEL
Country Music's Cajun Brothers

JODY MAPHIS
Noted Nashville Guitarist

B. B. MORSE
*Bass & Vocals for Freddy Powers
President of Reno's Blues Society*

FREDDY POWERS CELEBRITY GOLF TOURNAMENT & SHOW
1995
Special Olympics Nevada

Bump & Grind

Butch McMurtry
1946-1978
Bump & Grind

1972 **rock beat**

By JERRY BLEDSOE
Those of you who enjoy a driving back beat or the growl of an electric guitar, or even just a hand clapping good time, read on.

Russ Thompson, Butch McMurtry and Terry Harris owners and operators of the Daly Planet on Glendale Road... now appearing there are Goodlife, a talented local rock group Tuesday through Saturday, also cartoons on band breaks and a full length feature film every Tuesday from 8 to 10.

Bump & Grind

B.B. Morse

Local boogie band Bump and Grind doing Yori's concert

Reno's own country-boogie group, Bump and Grind, takes over the weekly concert chores Sunday-Tuesday, Aug. 24-26, at Yori's Disco 2000.

The seven-member group has been playing to full houses in the Lake Tahoe area since returning from a successful tour of Texas and the Southwest.

Bump and Grind specializes in a musical assortment of country-boogie, western swing and down-home funky music for dancing.

The group consists of Butch McMurtrey, lead singer, trombonist, banjoist and rhythm guitarist; Fred Meyers on drums, Scott Meyers on lead and side guitar, Doug Jones on lead guitar, Bob Fisher on trumpet, Randy Fisher on trombone and Bill Morris on bass. All do vocals, too.

Nightly festivities at Yori's begin around 10 a.m. and continue until dawn.

Between sets, Yori's own disco-DJ bar provides the music as well as during the rest of the week.

Coming next to the Kietzke Lane night spot is Stoneground for a special Labor Day Weekend engagement, Aug. 31-Sept. 1.

■ **Fort Reno,** the makeshift bivouac in the casino core, wraps up its 10 nights of musical entertainment this weekend.

The schedule: folk-rocker **Jesse Colin Young** ("Get Together"), tonight at 8 and 10:30; **Mark Lindsay** (Ex-Paul Revere/Raiders vocalist), 8 and 10:30 Saturday night; bar band/recording artists **Beat Farmers,** 8 and 10:30 Sunday night.

Reno's own **Bump & Grind** opens for the Beat Farmers. Tickets are $15 at the door for the first two acts, $12 for the Beat Farmers.   **1991**

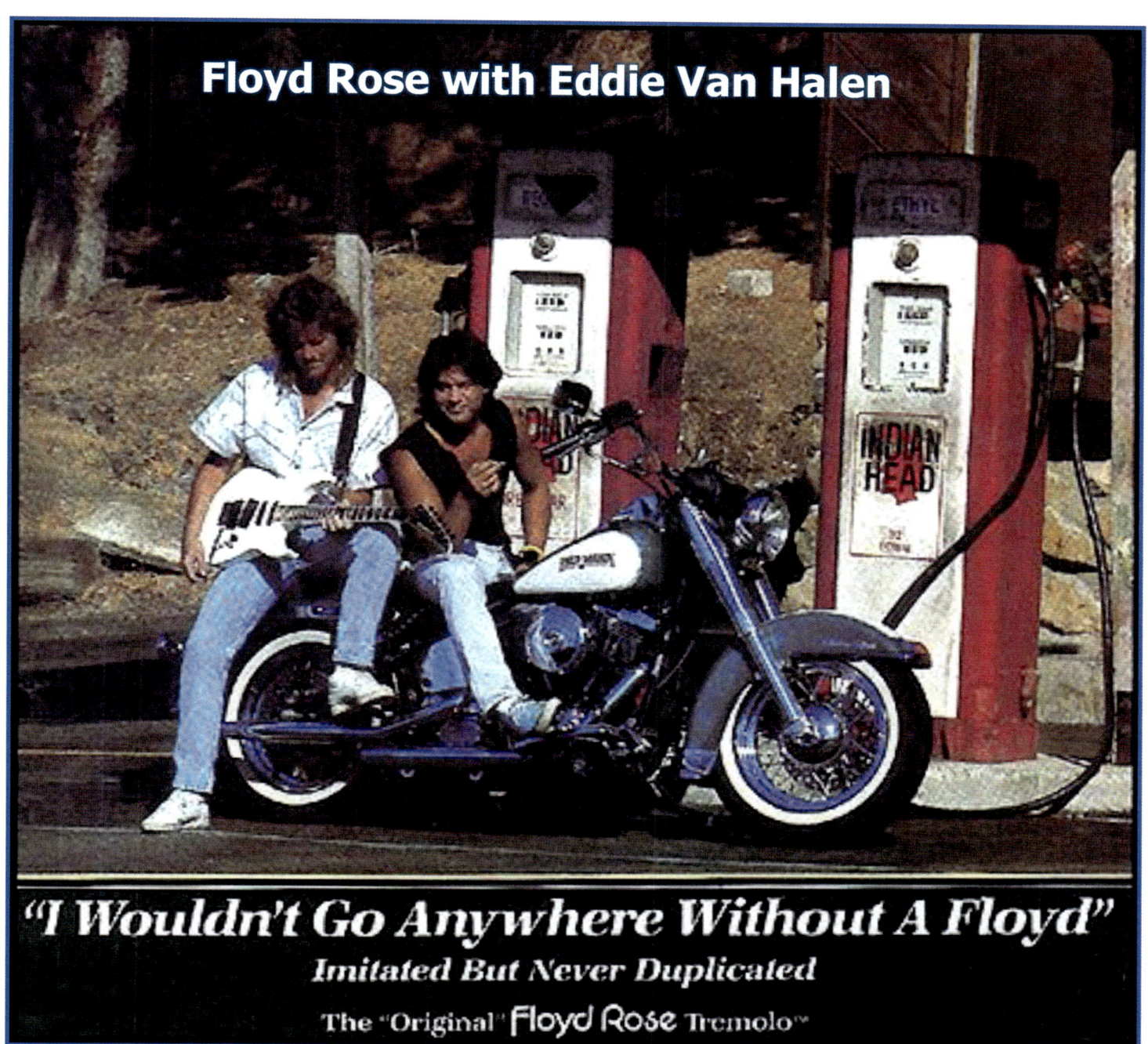

Floyd Rose with Eddie Van Halen

"I Wouldn't Go Anywhere Without A Floyd"
Imitated But Never Duplicated
The "Original" Floyd Rose Tremolo™

Reno's own Floyd Rose played in several Reno bands, such as "The Strangers", "Eclipse", and "Threshold", before inventing the Floyd Rose Locking Tremelo System. Every major rock guitarist applied it to their guitars, and the rest is history!

Rob Hanna

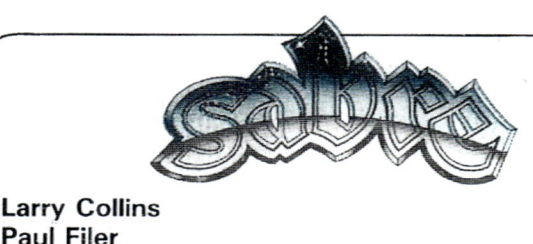
 **Takin' Care Of Business!**

Chuck Ruff
1951—2011

Guitar Woody and the Fly-By-Night Band, featuring the "Queen of Steam", Michele Lundeen

Guitar Woody & The Boilers with Michele Lundeen

G-Force

the lazy eights are a five-piece original rock band from Reno, Nevada. Over the past five years they have developed a unique sound—a combination of intelligent pop, alternative country, bluegrass and blues. Their energy and drive on stage make them a popular dance band, but their musicality and precision also satisfy those who just want to listen to good, innovative new music.

The Lazy Eights instantly won over the crowd. Because of their speed, fiddle and banjo, the Lazy Eights are often called a bluegrass band. Because of their drinking, love-gone-horribly-wrong songs, they could be considered country. But the overall impression they give is one of a jamming rock band. Their polished, high-energy set was a blast to watch. you owe it to yourself to seek out one of their many area shows.
RENO GAZETTE-JOURNAL

Speaking of bluegrass music, a new hybrid of the beast has come charging out of the west in the form of a band called The Lazy Eights.
MUSIC CONNECTION MAGAZINE

At any given performance fans of Reno's Lazy Eights twist, swing, jump around, two-step, and slam dance. Mostly, they smile. Rarely do they sit.
RENO NEWS AND REVIEW

BEN WILBORN

Ben provides lead vocals, violin, mandolin and acoustic guitar and writes the majority of the band's tunes. A graduate of Berklee School of Music in Boston, he has performed and recorded with such greats as Willie Nelson, Merle Haggard, Johnny Rodrigues, and Freddy Powers.

ROSS NICKERSON

Ross adds a distinctive and unique flavor with his one-of-a-kind Deering electric banjo. He has recorded with Riders in the Sky, Joe Craven, Darol Anger, and Tim O'Brien, to name a few, and has performed from Tokyo to Opryland, USA.

MIKE TILTON

Lead electric and acoustic guitar are provided by Mike, AKA "Mikey T" (it's a long story). He grew up on a rich diet of the Allman Brothers and Eric Clapton, as his hot solo work will attest.

JOEY McKINNEY

Joey holds the bottom down with his distinctive funky bass lines. Before the Lazy Eights, he played with Buzzard's Roost and the High Strung Band. In his spare time he is a geophysicist, hence his nickname, "Uncle Science".

DEREK SMITH

Rounding out the quintet is Derek, who started touring as a professional drummer as soon as he emerged from the egg. He has played with Freddy Fender, The Boston Wranglers, and The Kimberleys, with whom he had a top radio hit in 1978.

the lazy eights

are a hard-working, professional band, playing as many as one hundred and fifty dates a year. Their second CD, *five eights*, has sold over two thousand copies and continues to gain airplay and sales throughout the west. Among their accomplishments are performances at the NXNW music conference in Portland, Oregon, and being voted "Reno's best band" for the past two years by the Reno News and Review readers' poll.

They have shared the stage with acts as diverse as Merle Haggard, Todd Snider, Buckwheat Zydeco, Mumbo Gumbo, Doug Kershaw and Jack Ingram. They consistently draw full houses in their Reno-Tahoe area shows.

283

Blues singer's career rollin' again

The late rock and blues legend **Janis Joplin** just plain couldn't sing when her music career began. That's the assessment of Reno blues singer **Angel South**, who graduated with her in 1961 from Thomas Jefferson High in Port Arthur, Texas.

Yet, as the ol' sayin' goes, practice makes perfect. South noticed a dramatic change in Joplin's singing a few years after her professional music career started. In the late 1960s, he invited her to appear with his 10-piece blues band in Dallas.

"She showed heart with her voice," said South, 53, born with the Cajun name Lucien Gondron.

Joplin and South became close friends. They last saw each a few years before she died from a heroin overdose on Oct. 4, 1970.

South was a guitar player for famed blues musician **Bill Chase**, who also died young. South missed a doomed plane flight that crashed Aug. 9, 1974, in Jackson, Minn., killing Chase and three members of Chase's band.

South

Now South's career has taken off again, thanks largely to his popular new song, "Heart Shaped Butt," about a man who wants a gal with such a posterior.

Produced by Hollywood Sound Recorders, "Butt" soared last fall to the top notch on Las Vegas blues radio, and it did well in limited-test marketing.

Encouraged by results, Cleveland-based Action Music snatched up the album. In mid-April, it will be sent to 1,700 East Coast music stores and 200 radio stations. Strong sales would widen distribution.

Beginning Monday, South will play weekdays from 12:30 to 4:30 p.m. at the Horizon hotel-casino, Stateline, Lake Tahoe. Admission is free.

■ ■ ■

Larry Yates & the Blues Monsters

T-Bone Stone gives the blues at Slaphappy's

By Wayne R. Melton
GAZETTE-JOURNAL

Slaphappy's, 1295 E. Second St., opened New Year's Eve, and it has already emerged as a popular nightly entertainment spot.

Image Blue is featured most Thursdays at Slaphappy's, Reno's newest nightclub and lounge.

T-Bone Stone & The Nightcrawlers also appears occasionally on Thursday nights.

Its entertainment schedule rotates on a nightly basis, often bringing in traveling bands for one-time appearances.

Friday's night's lineup, for instance, features the music group Dig — featured in videos on MTV.

And the first half of every other Saturday night's entertainment lineup usually features a male revue for an all-female audience. When the male revue ends, the door opens to male visitors, and popular or alternative CDs are played for late-night dancing action.

Headed by Troy "T-Bone" Stone, 44, the regular Thursday night band plays original Chicago blues. The group also is regularly featured at other local night clubs, including the Lookout at the South Lake Tahoe Airport.

The band recently released a CD titled "Live Bait" on the Alchemy label. And Stone said the band is scheduled for a Eu-

T-Bone Stone and the Nightcrawlers . . . Thursdays at Slaphappy's.

ropean performance tour starting in May.

"Mostly, our repertoire features older blues that bands don't do much anymore," Stone said. "We take the old '20s and '30s blues songs and bring them to the public again. Most audiences like what we do,

because they really don't get a chance to hear that music anymore."

Headed by harmonica player and singer Steve "Stevie Dee" King, Image Blue plays rhythm and blues, classic rock and soul.

Terry & The T-Birds

Perfect Circle

Tunes via a Perfect Circle at Fitz

They're called Perfect Circle.

And they're the perfect answer if you need some fun and entertainment.

Terry Gerard leads the popular group with her vocal stylings and keyboard mastery.

A former piano and voice teacher from Tucson, Ariz., Gerard was featured with several other top acts before joining Perfect Circle in Reno.

Kevin Tokarz and Gary Douglas first put together the Circle foursome in 1976 and have been playing showrooms and lounges from Las Vegas to Atlantic City ever since.

Tokarz is a vocalist who knows his way around the keyboards. His background includes stints at the Gaslight Club in his native Chicago where he developed a taste for jazz.

Gary Douglas is a jazz buff and a singer's singer. His intricate vocal harmonies have earned him the unofficial title of "vocal acrobat."

Douglas is no stranger to the stage, having begun his career as a child actor and ukulele player. Like Tokarz, he discovered jazz and soon switched to the guitar and bass.

Roger Hoinacki is the group's newcomer plucked from the funk-rock circuit in Chicago.

He adds the instrumental and vocal stylings that make Perfect Circle such a versatile listening pleasure.

To make any evening more perfect, catch Perfect Circle, appearing nightly, except Tuesdays, at Fitz-

ROUNDLY ENTERTAINING: Perfect Circle presents the tunes at Fitzgeralds' Ritz Showbar through June 14. Passion shares the spotlight starting June 1. No cover or minimum.

geralds Ritz Showbar from 9:30 p.m. — 3 a.m. through June 14.

Beginning June 1, Perfect Circle will share the stage with Passion.

The Passion ensemble performs from 3:30 — 9 p.m. each evening except Mondays.

There is no cover or minimum in the Ritz Showbar located on the first floor of Fitzgeralds in the heart of downtown Reno.

Terry Gerard

The Ultimates

6—ENTERTAINMENT, SEPT. 24, 1966
Reno Evening Gazette and Nevada State Journal

THE ULTIMATES, the Reno area's modern dancing aggregation, perform on Friday and Saturday nights in the Sky Room of the Mapes Hotel. In addition to the fine sounds of the Ultimates, the Sky Room offers the largest dance floor in the Reno area.

THE HOMESTEAD ACT
Elmo · Patsy Magnolia

Steve Hobson
Hacienda Del Sol
1989

Cheyenne

Bobby Dee & Company

Midnight Riders

Dave Rucilez

Savage proves versatility

Opening Sunday, May 9 at Reno's Ponderosa Hotel and Casino, is the Jan Savage Quartet. The versatile group will be in the Ponderosa Room through May 16. Opening Monday, May 17 for an indefinite engagement are the Esquires.

Leader Jan Savage plays piano, vibes, and vocalizes. She is no newcomer to Ponderosa audiences, having played in the Ponderosa Room regularly since the hotel's opening.

The versatile Jan Savage group doubles on many instruments playing selections from "businessman's bounce," blues and novelties to sophisticated rock to satisfy the most discriminate of listeners and dancers.

Jan Savage

Jan Savage and Bob Braman

Tony Savage and his Mom, Jan

289

Irrepressible Jan Savage enjoys herself at work

Jan Savage

Why does a pretty, talented and vibrant woman prefer to work when she doesn't have to?

Why doesn't she stay in her lovely home with her family and plants?

Why does she come out of retirement in order to smile sweetly, play the piano charmingly and entertain during the cocktail hour in the Mapes Coach Room Tavern?

Jan Savage has had it all ways. She has been at the top of her profession in the Reno area. At the age of 22, hers was a top lounge act in the large casinos in the area. She played the Mapes when Sammy Davis Jr. was upstairs in the Sky Room.

Before that she played at work (what is work, but the play of grown-ups). With her father, Louis Rasasco, she had performed professionally before audiences since she was 4. Her piano-playing, musicianship, cheerful personality and beauty had brought Miss Savage success and a feeling of achievement not enjoyed by many women.

Then, at the height of her career, she turned to the pleasant life at home. So why, after four years in retirement, did she need to "come back?"

"People," she said.

"I like people and know almost everyone in town. I'm terrible on names but I never forget their favorite tune."

She continued enthusiastically, "in doing a single you have to be liked for yourself. Before they can like what you do they have to like who you are and what you represent. It's fun when old friends come into the Coach Room and say, 'You look great — How've you been?' "

The Mapes Coach Room fits Jan perfectly because it is so "intimate and friendly. It's the only place in Reno that has some action at the cocktail hour."

When asked about her singing ability and musicianship, Miss Savage shrugged and described herself as a "stylist."

"I do the best I can," she smiled. "You know — you try. You just try."

And Jan Savage, who has been "trying" all her life, has passed on this will to succeed to her young son, Tony Savage, 18. Tony with his drums and superb musicianship, is well on his way.

"He can play all types of music," she said. "Sometimes he plays with me and my group, but he has his own career.

"He's really a 'Show Musician.' He's great."

That's exhuberant Jan Savage, happy with her life, happy with her family and happy with her job at the Mapes.

TONY SAVAGE
musician

Tony Savage knows what it's like to be at the top of his profession. As an 18-year-old out of Wooster High School, Savage went on a 12-year world tour as Engelbert Humperdinck's drummer. He performed at famous venues such as Royal Albert Hall in London, Carnegie Hall, Radio City Music Hall and throughout Australia. "I got paid to see the world," Savage said. "But it was a real abrupt awakening."

So much so that, amidst personal problems, Savage quit the band. "I think everyone hits bottom at some time in their life," he said. "I decided to come back home to Reno and pull myself out."

And so he did. Now, he has his own band — the Tony Savage Trio — which plays at Adele's at the Plaza Friday and Saturday nights. The trio released a Christmas album last December and Savage expects to do another album later this year. Savage is also engaged to a local nurse, Linda Hubert. "I'm happy now," he says. "I feel lucky to be able to develop (the talent) God has given me."
— *Neil Baron/photo by Jean Dixon Aikin*

Success Story

Success story nominations: 324-0225, code 4663

RENO GAZETTE-JOURNAL

SIERRA Life

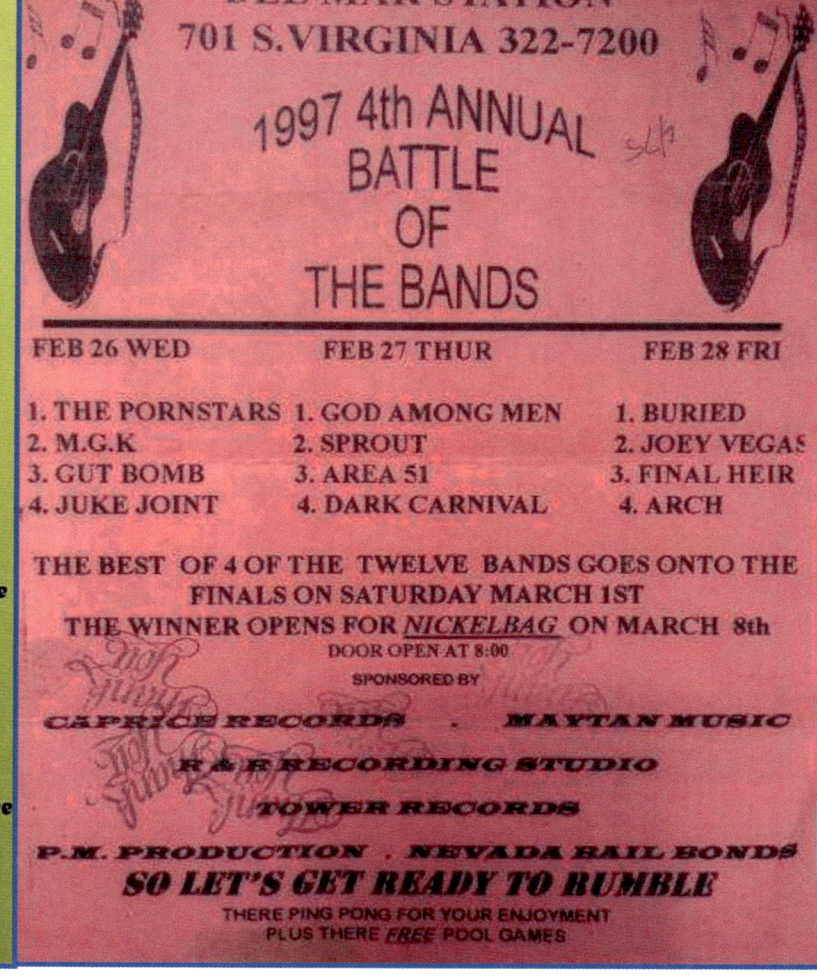

The Band:

Brian 'B.Z.' Zeleniak: Lead Guitars, Vocals, Harmonica

Wayne 'Z' Zeleniak: Rhythm Guitars, Vocals, Keyboards

John 'Buzzard' Reid: Bass Guitars, Vocals

Mitch 'The Bitch' England: Drums, Vocals

The Band started in 1993 as an original project with the sole intent of recording. However, the enthusiasm expressed by everyone who heard the band prompted them to start going public in late 1994. Every member of the group has an extensive musical background which is apparent in their playing. They have succeded in becoming one of the best bands in the area in a very short period of time. A big part of their success has been in their selection of material, the best of the major groups, as well as their own originals which have proven to be very competetive in the Rock world.

DEL MAR STATION
701 S. VIRGINIA 322-7200

1997 4th ANNUAL
BATTLE
OF
THE BANDS

FEB 26 WED	FEB 27 THUR	FEB 28 FRI
1. THE PORNSTARS	1. GOD AMONG MEN	1. BURIED
2. M.G.K	2. SPROUT	2. JOEY VEGAS
3. GUT BOMB	3. AREA 51	3. FINAL HEIR
4. JUKE JOINT	4. DARK CARNIVAL	4. ARCH

THE BEST OF 4 OF THE TWELVE BANDS GOES ONTO THE
FINALS ON SATURDAY MARCH 1ST
THE WINNER OPENS FOR *NICKELBAG* ON MARCH 8th
DOOR OPEN AT 8:00
SPONSORED BY
CAPRICE RECORDS . MAYTAN MUSIC
R & R RECORDING STUDIO
TOWER RECORDS
P.M. PRODUCTION . NEVADA BAIL BONDS
SO LET'S GET READY TO RUMBLE
THERE PING PONG FOR YOUR ENJOYMENT
PLUS THERE *FREE* POOL GAMES

Starr Donaldson with...

Joe Richards Group 1980

Jo Jo Gunne, 1974

Joe Richards Group

Opera, 1976

Sawbuck was a San Francisco band that featured three of Reno's finest musicians...Chuck Ruff, Bill Church, and Starr Donaldson. The other two members shown here are Mojo Collins (upper left), and Ronnie Montrose (far right). They signed with Fillmore Records and released an album in 1972.

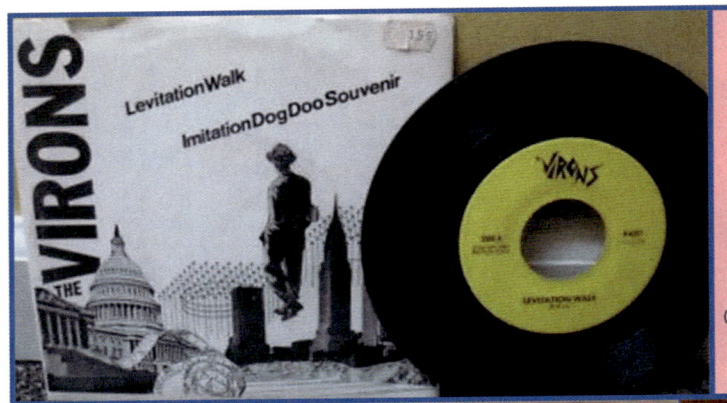

THE VIRONS
Levitation Walk
Imitation Dog Doo Souvenir

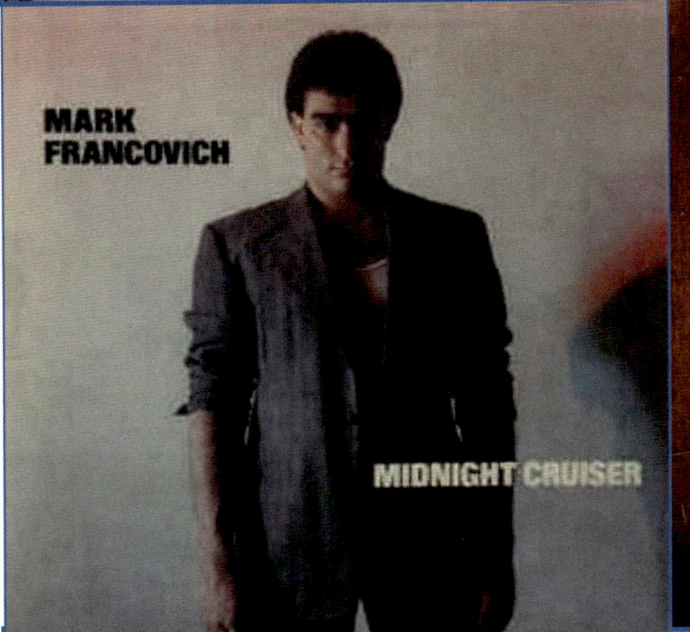

MARK FRANCOVICH

MIDNIGHT CRUISER

Live Music
Fri & Sat. Nite
10:00 P.M. Till ?
Diggers Saloon
624 B St. Sparks
356-9543
Presents
Kelly's Boogie Band

The Edgar Winter Group

Shock Treatment

Autographed by the band!

DALE KENNEDY

Jim Kinn

Greg Sample

HALLOWEEN PARTY

COSTUME REQUIRED

COSTUME REQUIRED

at "Memorial Hall" th
October 26
8 p.m. to 2 a.m.
Point Blank Promotion
Presents LIVE
Sabre
$4.00

Admissions : In advance
At the door : $5.00
Prizes for the top 3 costumes
will be awarded at:10:00pm

No one under 18 —Tickets At— "Electronic Butterfly"

BULLET

at the
DIRECT CONNECTION
Carson City's hotest night club

FRIDAY & SATURDAY NIGHT
FEBRUARY 24 & 25

*Come and dance to Reno's
new sound in ROCK!*

Whyte Widow

BEST BETS

A guide to the people, places and pleasures of Reno, Tahoe, Sparks & Carson

May 16 – 22, 1991

Cover story

May 16-22, 1991 — Reno Gazette-Journal

Nightlife outside the casinos

Two local semi-pro bands prep for stardom

By Michael Sion
GAZETTE-JOURNAL

The five members of local band The Choice look like they embody the spectrum of current rock music:

The metalhead drummer's wearing black boots and pants decorated with the saying, "Kill City and Skulls." The hippy second guitarist has wire-frame glasses and a tie-dyed bandanna over his long hair. The bassist wears a black fedora, suit and eyeshades, like some bluesman. The vocalist is dressed like Huey Lewis in shirt, tie and jeans. And the Neil Young-looking lead guitarist has holes in his pant's knees, and a green tanktop that reads "The Choice."

"We're five separate bands in one," says lead guitarist, Rich Dugan.

Call them a "classic rock" band. One that plays everything from the Grateful Dead to Van Halen, INXS and their own originals.

And one in a handful of local semi-pro bands that have a healthy bar following.

Another is the Pods.

To classify this local trio is near-impossible.

The dark-haired drummer (Derek Smith) and bassist (Tom Melancon) form a tight rhythm section. But the centerpiece is the bald, distinctive-looking singer-guitarist, Dean Smith.

He plays "quarter-chords" — one chord per beat in the 4/4 time — which creates a galloping gait.

Dean Smith says it's like ska — or double-time reggae. But Derek Smith (no relation) terms the Pods' original repertoire "psycho-eclectic surfabilly."

"It's not your basic three-chord rockers, although it's very danceable," says Derek.

OK. Chances are you've never heard of the Pods. Or The Choice.

Chances are you don't get out much to non-casino nightlife venues.

But if you like rock 'n' roll, and you support local music, those are two of the names you should remember from the present, burgeoning local music scene.

Yes, there IS nightlife outside the casinos. And the local semi-pro music scene continues to rock, roll and reverberate this weekend.

We mention the Pods and The Choice because they are two fine bands playing this weekend in local clubs.

The Choice — guitarists Dugan and Chip Billharz, drummer Greg Sample, bassist Mark Palmer and vocalist Stephen King — play every weekend, and sometimes add a couple midweek dates.

They're booked three months in advance. And while it's tough to earn a C-note per member on a gig, they feel fortunate to have a following, which they say is part-Deadhead, part blue-collar.

"A lot of people say we're cheesy, sometimes. But we *work all the time*, and a lot of people are envious," says King.

The Choice plays the Beer Barrel, Stein of the Times, Zephyr Bar, Icehouse, Tumbleweed Bar, Good Time Charlie's and the 89th Street Bar and Grill in South Lake Tahoe.

"We base our set list around the crowd," says Sample. "Slam 'em if it's a party crowd."

"If it's a listening crowd, we hit them with 'Elizabeth Reed,'" says Dugan.

"If it's a dance crowd, we hit 'em with five or six rock 'n' roll songs."

WHERE TO FIND
LOCAL SEMI-PRO BANDS
- **The Pods**: 10 p.m. Friday at the Tumbleweed Bar & Grill, 1295 E. Second St.
- **The Choice**: 10 p.m. Friday and Saturday at the venerable Icehouse Saloon, 310 Spokane Street.

The Pods play about every other week.

They do some cover songs — including some old numbers from the legendary local band the Smiths were in, the Boston Wranglers (which still plays an infrequent date). But the Pods favor originals.

The Pods' barroom "hits" include "Sex Party," "Ride Around the World," "Tons of Time," "Voodoo Doll of You" and "When is Grandma Gonna Die?"

Says Derek: "Our songs tend to exploit the . . ."

"Weak and helpless," says Dean, finishing the sentence.

The Smiths say their fans range from 45-year-old eccentrics to 21-year-old airheads.

"President Bush probably wouldn't want to see us," says Derek.

"*He* might," says Dean.

"There's a small, select, hip population to support us," he says.

Overall — Reno live music buffs are barhoppers, says The Choice's Dugan. Fans can hit five or six clubs on a weekend night, he says.

"I think they're frustrated," says vocalist King.

"When they find the Choice, we try to fit to them."

And when they find the Pods — their bodies might be snatched onto the dance floor.

Greg Sample, "Citizen"
Guam, 1988

Greg and Kevin Sample
"Radiant", 1976

Xavier

Paisley Brain Cells

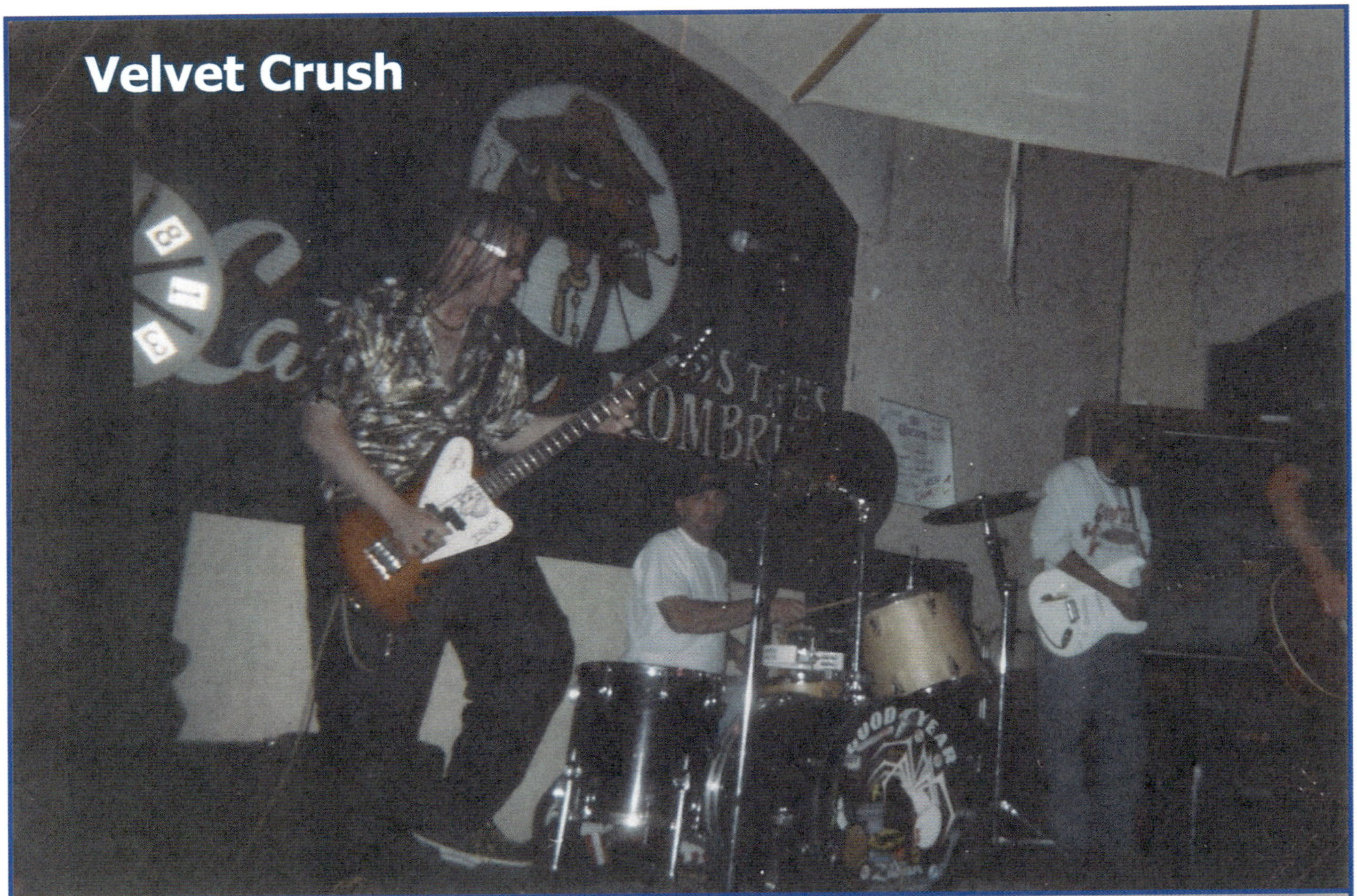
Velvet Crush

12-Nevada Appeal, Carson Chronicle—Wednesday, June 25, 1980

Amethysis

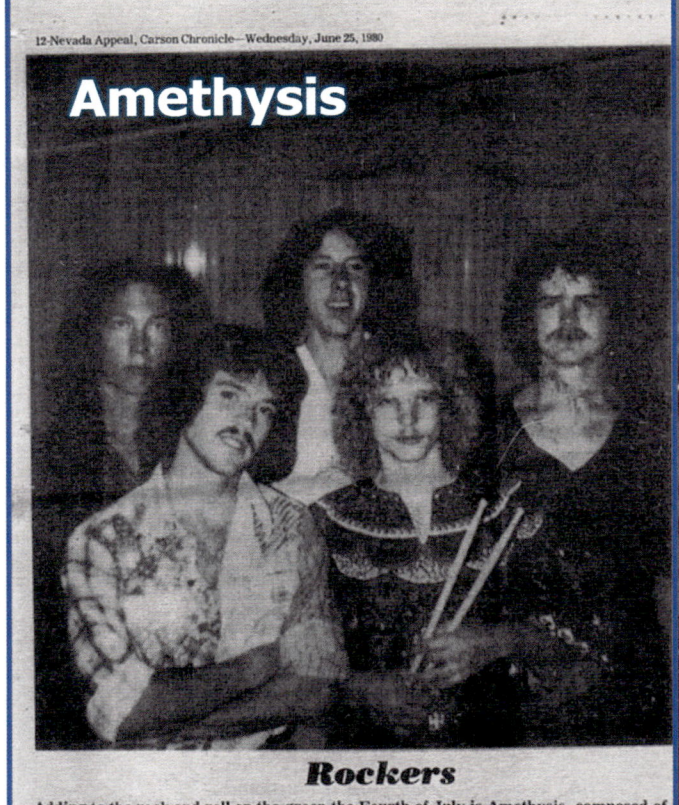

Rockers

Adding to the rock and roll on the green the Fourth of July is Amethysis, composed of, left, Bill Grow, Kevin Cox, Jeff Miller, Steve Vecchiarelli and Danny Farmer. They played at Backstreet.

Danny George
"Mr. Rhythm"

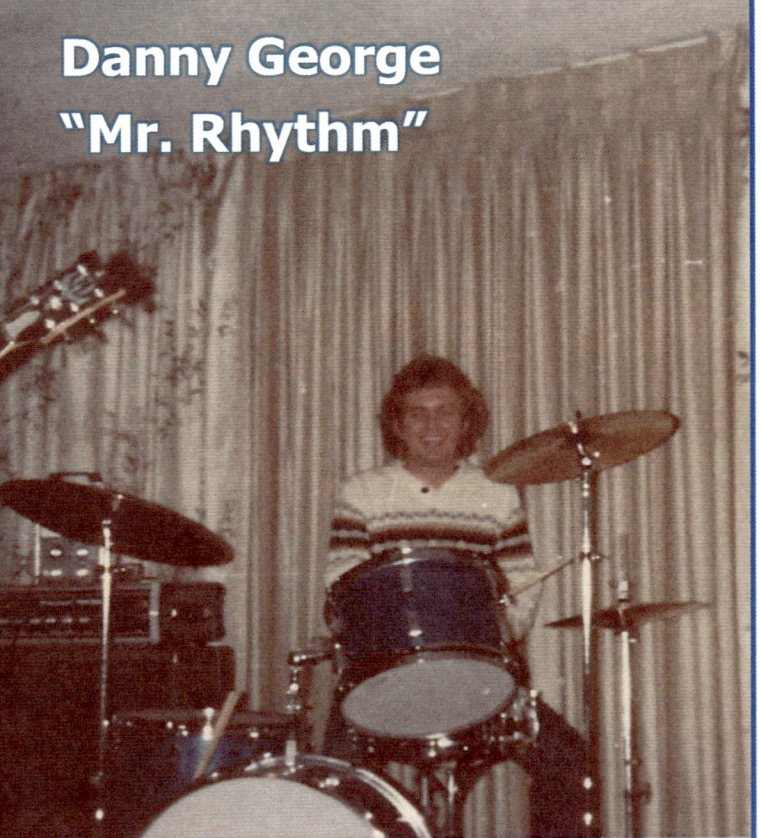

Taxi soup to nuts for Reno's rock and roll appetite

By JIM NEWMAN

Reno is basically on a starvation diet when it comes to rock and roll. Between the occasional concerts booked into town, many rock fans rely on several of Reno's own bands for entertainment.

Some are good, and others aren't. Taxi, however, is a standout. With this group, Reno has a reputable, professional entry into the rock industry.

Taxi's biggest advantage is that it has a stable of songs that are not only original, but very good.

Friday evening, a small — yet receptive — crowd gathered at a former country music club, The Hayloft on Wells Avenue, to listen to Taxi grind out its impressive array of tunes. Many of the fans are repeat customers for the group.

Taxi's second advantage is leader Gilbert Trujillo, a young songwriter who handles guitar and singing chores. The band also includes Dan George on drums, Bob McNamarra on bass, and Bobby Crewz on rhythm guitar and Michael Manning on keyboards.

Trujillo has a good voice that adapts well to material by many popular contemporary artists — Eagles, Cars, Toto — in addition to Taxi's own songs.

Trujillo's original music includes "She Loves To Be In Love," "Baby Please Have A Heart,"

"But Baby" and probably Taxi's best entry, "Make a New Plan."

These tunes have a sophistication that eludes many local groups. The band's execution of the music is clean and tasteful.

Taxi is also big on Eagles tunes such as "The Long Run" and "The Greeks Don't Want No Freaks." They come as close to the originals as possible.

Although enjoyable and apparently hard-working, Taxi has a problem: it lacks balanced talent. The group is centered entirely around songwriter and master showman Trujillo. Without him, the group would be lost.

Attempts at brilliance by other players just don't match his efforts. Keyboardist Manning, for example, occasionally throws in some fancy electronics, only to have the Cars song "She's My Best Friend's Girl" sound like the theme from "Star Wars."

Could the band find a way to match Trujillo, they could open a major concert in town.

The band has loosened up since previous visits to the Hayloft, but with Trujillo's exception they still offer only a mediocre stage show.

Jim Newman, rock critic for the Gazette and Journal, is a student at the University of Nevada-Reno.

Sidro's Armada

Sidro's Armada sets sail at Harrah's Reno

Sidro's Armada, an eight-piece, highly energized rock 'n' roll band, shakes the Casino Cabaret at Harrah's Reno nightly, except Tuesdays, through April 6.

The band's material runs the musical gamut from rock 'n' roll to rhythm and blues. They perform original compositions as well as songs of other performers including Lionel Richie's "All Night Long," Tina Turner's "What's Love Got To Do With It?" and Rickie Lee Jones' "Easy Money."

"We have the ability to make a musical left turn at a moment's notice," says Sidro Garcia, lead guitarist and band leader. "After the first two or three songs we change to suit each audience."

Sidro's Armada also features lead singer Beverly Brown, Louis Leos on bass, Steve Ingham on drums, and Daryl Wainscott on keyboards and synthesizer. The brass section features Sal Ricardo, Kevin Stout and Tom Frazee.

"Sidro Garcia is an incredible guitarist," one critic noted. "In one of his own compositions, he goes from slow, plaintive melody to speeds so fast the eye cannot follow his fingers — all without missing a beat."

Sidro's Armada alternates on the Cabaret stage with the pioneer rock 'n' roll group the Clovers through March 22, and with Rain: A Tribute to the Beatles March 29 through April 5.

For show times call 329-4422.

Paul Revere tops list of Reno music award winners

By Mark Crawford/Gazette-Journal

With emcee and double award winner Paul Revere (and some of his Raiders) heading the list, 33 local and world entertainment acts took home Reno Area Music Award (RAMA) trophies after ceremonies at the Grand Ballroom.

The rock 'n' roll nightclub was nearly packed Monday night with 500 invited artists, technicians, producers, media people and friends for the second annual series of awards in music and comedy from the past year's Reno-Tahoe scene.

Nominations were by popular ballot. From four finalists in each category, a panel of six judges (musicians, technicians and executives) chose a 1985 "favorite." The favorite act should not be assumed the "top" or "best," said director Cathy Johnson, who produced the event with Starsound Productions and the Ballroom.

Eligible acts must have played at least two nights in Reno in 1985 and must not have signed recording contracts. (Casino headliners and one-time superstar concerts were exempt.)

Revere, who co-emceed the awards with KRNO-FM and KOLO-TV broadcaster Dave Finley, repeatedly said "That's incredible!" as he accepted the Hall of Famer award over nominees Red Skelton and Lelands chief Lee Henricksen.

While insisting "we used our own best judgment at the time," Johnson acknowledged the appearance of several conflicts of interest. Her husband, country fiddler and guitarist Christian Johnson, had been nominated but did not win. One judge, rock keyboardist and Starsound engineer Mark Ishikawa, also was a nominee. Although Ishikawa did not win, a former member of his Sugarfoot band did win.

Johnson said future judge panels would be expanded.

Winning casino headliners were Bill Cosby, main room; Revere, cabaret act; B. B. King, individual cabaret performer; Williams and Ree, comedians; and Hi-Heeled Sneakers, cabaret revue.

Concert winners were Yes, rock; Alabama, country; Spyro Gyra, jazz. The KOZZ-FM Hotline won a media award.

Other winners:

Leo Swift, rock group; Montana Band, country group; Jimmy Cicero Trio, jazz group; Michelle Rohl, female rock singer; Carl Driggs, male rock singer; Cheryl Cotton, female country singer; Terry Robinson, male country singer; Lucy Lucille, female jazz singer; Jimmy Cicero, male jazz singer.

Rock instrumentalists: Steve Hobson, guitar; Danny Krause, keyboards; Dave Wicks, bass; Danny Cruces, drums.

Country instrumentalists: Kurt Bergeron, guitar; Jimmy Boggio, keyboards; Alan Larson, bass; Johnny Podash, fiddle; Mark Wittman, drums.

Jazz instrumentalists: Sid Jacobs, guitar; Bill Anderson, keyboards; Danny Leoni, bass; John Gronberg, horns; Steve Self, drums.

Jerry Bledsoe

Manzanita Jungle

Steven Erich Schweizer   1951-2018

The Bands, and others...

What follows is a listing of bands, musicians, and entertainers who are featured in this book. We have endeavored, through days, weeks, and months of research... interviews, newspaper and magazine articles, band biographies, phone conversations, and by word of mouth...to present a complete as possible compilation of the hundreds of such players.

Yes, some will be incomplete. In a few instances, non-existent.

When perusing this section, we ask that you take into consideration the many factors that make such a venture virtually impossible with regard to perfection.

The passage of time. The faded memories. The lack of documentation. Misinformation from sources. Indifference. And yes, sadly, even death.

Even so, if you've shown an interest in reading this, we're certain that you will recognize many of the names put forth here.

Many achieved not only a modicum of fame in the Reno area...some went on to national recognition.

We, the authors, are indeed proud to present to you these many memories of days, friends, and music past...in the hope that it will conjure images of the many happy times we spent dancing, partying, laughing, and...uh...in some cases singing along (with varying degrees of intonation!) with these multi-talented people.

Band, Group, Performer Name	Band, group Member(s)	Page Number(s)
2nd Coming	Lou Allard, Curry Jameson, Mark McGuire	110, 182
7 Seconds	Steve Youth, Kevin Marvelli, Troy Mowat, Bobby Adams	161
702	Rick Hokenson, Pete Eckart, Mark McPhail, Richard Washburn	255
Act, The	Larry Goldman, Richard Washburn, Bob Gardener, Nancy Gardener	254
A' La Mode	Steve Hatley, Terry Petersen, Jerry Bledsoe, Starr Donaldson, Jerry Kratzmeyer, Bob Ciarcia, Steve Dunwoodie, Denny Phelps, Ken Steimonts, Jerry Weems, Rob Hanna, Steve Hobson, Steve Self, Bimmie Bjornsen, Paul Geise	91, 92, 253
Amazon Grace	Doug Goddard, Dave Kidd, Paul Manktelow, Herman H.	164
Amethysis	Bill Grown, Kevin Cox, Jeff Miller, Steve Vecchiarelli, Danny Farmer	300
Angel South	Angel South	284
Area 51	Brian Zeleniak, Wayne Zeleniak, Mitch England, John Reed	291
Avalanche	Rick Schultze, Danny Quintana, Gene Thorpe	90
B.B. & The Boomers	B.B. Morse, Michele Lundeen, Joel Edwards, Rene Best, Freddie Powers Jr., Derek Smith, George Pelham	272, 273
Baba Tao	Kandas Siren (Myer), Joseph Riley, Peter Damien Gutkowski, Bobbie Hamilton	182
Band on the Run	Dave Campanaro, Vic Campanaro, Greg Patelzick, Tab Warwick	57
Bandana	Paul Manktelow, Kandas Myer, Jeff Wiggs, Scott Gregory, Ron Ryser, Michael Opton	165
Bangalore Choir	John Kirk, Curtis Mitchell, Ian Mayo, Jackie Ramos, Danny Greenberg, Rene Letters, David Reece, Andy Susemihi, Hans in 't Zandt	55, 229
Blind Date	Rick Pike, John Sanchez, Randy Fleeman, Ron Houston, Jerry Coleman	258
Bobby Dee and Company	Bobby Dee, John Ponzo, Garry Pranin, Huck Lottman, Dave Rucilez	111, 288
Boxer	Terry Petersen, Michael Furlong, Rich Haines, Art Galvan, Jerry Kratzmeyer, Steve Hobson	120, 241

Broken Promise	Jerry Spikula, Danny Farmer, James Isham	250
Brother Me	Lou Werlinger, etc.	181
Browne Rice	Wayne Browne, Terry Rice, Mel Birch	145
Bullet	Paul Filer, Larry Collins, Craig Finsley, Jeff Lehmann, Greg Sample	295
Bump & Grind	Butch McMurtrey, B.B. Morse, Gary Joe Wade, Randy Fisher, Rookie Fisher, Scotty Paul Meyers, John Bernard	79, 273-276
Candymen, The	Bill Brown, Dennis Lord, Tom Donnelly, Gary Smith, Bob Lani	114
Cheryl Cotton Band	Cheryl Cotton, Joseph DeRosa, Ron Rummage, Jammey Kidd	93-96
Cheyenne	Remmel Wilson, Mike Gotcher, Randy Glasgow, Dave Rucilez, James Gernandt, Ernie Hagar	288
Chipped Beef on Toast	Joe McGuire, Casey Mulgrew, Lou Werlinger	180
Choice, The	Stephen King, Rich Dugan, Chip Billharz, Greg Sample, Mark Palmer	296
Chris Talbot	Chris Talbot	89
Chuck Ruff Group	Chuck Ruff, Jerry Kratzmeyer, Jerry Weems, Rick Pike, David Strelz, Steve Whitman, Randy Fleeman, Shanimal, Greg Golden, Jack White, Red Dawn, Johnny Hammons, John Sanchez, Terry Petersen, Ruben Von Ruden	130, 257, 259, 279
Citizen	Jay Morford, Jody Piper, Greg Sample, Scott Pelham	298
Cleveland	Glen Williams, Dave Sifritt, Mike Sankovich, Bryce Schill	191
Collins Kids, The	Larry Collins, Laurie Collins	147
Cork Proctor	Cork Proctor	263
Country Playboys	Kenny Rost, Kenny Lowrey, Jack Farell, Tommy Roscoe	186
Craig Evans Trio	Craig Evans, Kenny Dotson, John Whitney	70
Crazy 8's		145
Crazy Texas Gypsies	Jerry Coleman, Steve Hatley, Kenny Williams, Kevin Fraser	61
Crusader Rabbit	John Sanchez, Ron Barron, Johnny Hammons, Tom Evans, Chuck Ruff	28
Crystal Axe	Chris Crawford, Steve Steward, Paul Vasina, Greg Rose	149, 188
Crystal Image	Blair Booth, Dorlan Peckham, Louis Basso, Kurt Conkey, Steve ?	97
Dale Kennedy	Dale Kennedy	294
Dalton, Lacy J.	Lacy J. Dalton	153

Danny Marona	Danny Marona	262
Decker	Rob Hanna, Boris Tavcar, Bobby Nichols, Johnny Hammons, Michael Furlong	119
Decoys, The	Lou Werlinger, Ray Rodarte, Bill Campbell	174, 180, 192
Dedly Biznes	Johnny Hammons, Tommy Evans, Darren Britton, David Britton, Tony ?	71
Denny Long	Denny Long, Doug Cecil	185
Dogs, The	Jeff Barbagelata, Tom Glogovic, Dave Koliah, Rian Swift, Gary Elam	148
E Ticket	Steve Dunwoodie, Ken Valentine, Dennis Collins, Jim Costa	111
Easy Street	C.T. Urbani, Glen Gillette, Mike Wise	
Eclipse	Floyd Rose, Greg Golden, Lou Werlinger, Dennis Sublett	162
Eddie and the Cruisers	Lou Werlinger, Larry Goldman, Tracy Bing	192
Elijah	Steve Hobson, Danny Quintana, Jeff Dick, Gary Leach	112
Esquires, The	Bob Hanna, Joe Martini, Eddie Bee	226
Ethyl Myrtz	Mark Anthony, Dennis McGarvey, Nigel St. Hubbins, Steve Hatley	113
Family Portrait	Jerry Estes, Jim Estes, Jackie Estes, Ernie Hagar, Herman Hilkma, Steve Clarke	252
Fat Chance	Tom Donnelly, Rick Rudd, John Anderson, Scott Viggo, Ron Brown, John Van Emmerik, Bill Brown	116
Fiver	Rod MacKay, Paul Geise, Floyd Rose, Perry White, Steve Hobson, Donnie Anderson	190, 251
Flashback	Spud Ivens, Tami Ivens, Ted Nelson, Dan Robbins, Reba Poole, Kirk Poole	178
Foolish Behaviour	Mike Mantor, Al Wilkins, Steve Hobson, Randy Fleeman, John von Nolde, Michael Kelley, Jerry Weems, Jerry Coleman, Mark Campbell, and a cast of dozens!	98, 156, 159, 220, 237, 255
Frenz	Steve Cowart, Doug Cowart, Jeff Neiman, Kris Landrum, Steve Grantham	75, 76, 160
Frog Rock	Rick Pike, Skip Gillette, Steve Schweizer	246
G-Force	Jonnie G., Rich Carlson, James "Rooster" Olsen, Darrel Ogawa, Todd Skaw, Eddie Hosmer	282
Gary and Sandy, aka Gary & Sandy's Common Ground, aka Gary Raffanelli & Sandy Selby	Gary Raffanelli, Sandy Selby, Dave Clark, Tom White, Babe Pace, and many others!	63-69

Johnathan Goodlife	Steve Dunwoodie, Jerry Weems, Jim Mask, Jim Stipech, Rick Pike, Steve Schweizer	154
Johnny Slick and The Cheaters	Lou Werlinger Traci Bing, Bill Campbell, Ray Rodarte, Rudy Rodarte, Rick Lopez	143, 172, 173, 181
Judy Lynn Show	Judy Lynn and various sidemen!	111
Justice V/Justus V	Mike Mantor, Paul Manktelow, Steve Hatley, Ron Ryser, Kootch Trochim, Bill Church, Billy Ray Payne	17, 131, 154, 163
Kay Martin & Her Bodyguards	Kay Martin, Bill Elliott, Jess Hotchkiss, Tony Bellson, Buddy Raymond	226
Kelly's Boogie Band	William Kelly, Mark Word, Ted Argo, Richard Rowe	72, 294
Kenny Laursen Band, aka Kelly and the Cruisers (on occasion)	Kenny Laursen, Al Wilkins, Mary Petrowitz, Rick Pike, B.B. Morse, Teri Laursen	38-41
Kenny Stahl and Friends	Kenny Stahl, Brent Zane, John Wheeler	191
Kidds, The	John Sanchez, Randy Fleeman, Rick Pike, Mitch England, Bobby Nichols	259
Kimberlys	Harold Gaye, Carl Gaye, Ted Gaye, Verna Gaye, Michael Gaye, Curt Shultse, Terry Gaye, Richard Washburn	254
Lacy J. Dalton	Lacy J. Dalton	153
Larry & The Radicals	Buddy Shlosser, Dave Lindsay, John Espil, Larry Mullen	80
Larry Yates & the Blues Monsters	Larry Yates, Barry Slayton, Chuck Dunn, Michael Overhauser, Tom Barnes	284
Laura St. Romain	Laura St. Romain, Clyde Sutton, Jonathan Barton, Rick Yarrison, Brian Morgan, Joe Mendoza, Marc Dyson, Russ Letizia	137
Lazy Eights	Ben Wilborn, Ross Nickerson, Mike Tilton, Joey McKinney, Derek Smith	283
Lewd Vagrancy	Dave Jorda, Eric Bogumil, Eric Alvarez, Mike Melo	267
Links, The		185
Local 205, The	John Sanchez, Blake Storey, Jim Sargent, Kim Olsen, Pat Snyder	257
Local 420	Greg Rose, Jerry Davis, Zsolt Orose, Paul Vasina, Byron Jones	150, 188
Look, The	Dana Cowen, Rick Cowan, Brian Morgan, Vince Chappele	81-82
Los Huevos	Lou Werlinger, Ray Rodarte, Rick Lopez, Victor Lopez, Pam ?	174-175
Lost & Found, The	Mike McMullen, Tom Donnelly, Charlie Adams, Mike Ellis, John Van Emmerick	114
Lost and Found Dept.	Chuck Ruff, Stuart Schweizer	144

Petty Theft	Michael Furlong and a cast of dozens!	122
Pods, The	Derek Smith, Tom Melancon, Dean Smith	296
Power House	Fred Champoux, Kevin Strawn	250
Precious Metal	D.J. Lowman, Roger Ellis, Don Adult, Tabb Shackleton, Scott Holcomb, Geoffrey Wash	59
Project Bellvue	Tammy McNeil, Kevin Pate, Marie Sherwood, Danny Farmer, Paul Wolfe, Bruce ?	249
Radiant	Jeff Lehmann, Kevin Sample, Greg Sample	298
Rain (Reno Edition)	Joey Curatolo, Jim Riddle, Joe Bithorn, Ralph Castelli, Mark Lewis	134-136
Rawkon	Mark Grover, Mike Grover, Harold Crook, Guy Johnson, Pete Amato	42-44
Rayge	Ron Barron, Shannon Sullivan, Jeff Lehmann, Scott Taylor	60, 236
RazorMaid	Curt Mitchell, John Kirk, Dean Clarkson, Jim "Jamie Lee" Garrett, Dave Wix, Joe Gimabroni, Tom Lamb, Mike Moran, John Morris	29-30
Red Dawn	Kenny Williams, Lou Werlinger, Dawn, Drew	179, 259, 279
Renegade	"Big E" Erick Patterson, Andrew Nobbs, Gary Marsh'e, Walter Eastwood, Grant Cunningham, Lori Shaw, Terry "T-Bone" Cuppett	304
Revolver	Lee Miles, Mike Biselli, Bob Rasner, Ron Coder, Gary Fritz, Manuel Huentez	151
Rob Hanna's Salute to Rod Stewart	A cast of dozens!	119, 121, 155, 157, 158, 159, 160, 164
Rock Blvd.	Jim Olsen, Steve Hurd, Jim Gmur, Doug Jones	49
Ron Butler	Ron Butler	185
Rusty Butz	Michael Furlong, Naunie Furlong, Bill Campbell, Joe LaChew, Lou Werlinger, Ray Rodarte, Steve Hatley, Jerry Weems, Jim Honyumptewa	129, 174, 177, 181, 279
RV's. The	Michael Clark, Damon Henderson, Tom Ward, Chris Loomis	
Sables	Randy Banks, Tim Wrenn, Joe Espic	80
Sabre	Jeff Lehmann, Greg Sample, Larry Collins, Craig Finsley and Paul Filer	235, 279, 295
Saddle Tramps, The	John von Nolde, Scott Roller, Johnny Fingers, Suzi Switchblade, El Viagro (Mark Ashworth), Mike Mantor, Mike Young, Elijah Trotsky, John Perry	101-102

Sailor's Farm	Asgur Jorgensen, Kelly Kakes, Paul Mankte-low	167
Sanchez-Gillette-Loomis Band	John Sanchez, Skip Gillette, Chris Loomis	28
Satchmo	Michael Furlong, Nannie Furlong, Brent Har-pham, Lenar Gousetis, Richard Ray	119, 129
Sawbuck	Chuck Ruff, Bill Church, Starr Donaldson, Mojo Collins, Ronnie Montrose	293
Scratch	Brian Morgan, Perry Dunlap, Lee Fusco, Bob McNamara, Gilbert Trujillo	53
Shades, The	Lon Sygit, John Lundemo, Dave Koliha, Bud Goud	227
Shades of Blue	Michael Furlong, Jim Honyumptewa, Jim Johns, Jack Randell, Mike Giordano	118, 127
Sharks	Gary Joe Wade, Dean Wade, Gary Smith, Steve Dunwoodie, Mike Mantor	70
Ship of Fools	Rob Hanna, John Harmon, Matt Enser, John Lewis, Tom Lipzanski, Rick Yancey, Alan Lar-son, Linda ?	86-87
Sidro's Armads	Sidro Garcia, Beverly Brown, Louis Leos, Steve Ingham, Daryl Wainscott, Sal Ricardo, Kevin Stout, Tom Frazee	301
Silent Partner	Dana Cowen (Gutenberger), Mark Maxson, Bob Vetromile, Scott House, Bob Roth, Doug Fitts, Rick Cowen	81
Sin City	Jerry Coleman, John Sanchez, Will Houts, Dean Lowman, Jack White	117
Skid Kids	Danny Quintana,	112
Sledd		150, 188
Smoking Caterpillars	Bill Blackley, Tim Holst, Mark Frybarger, Greg Darnell, Ned Chaney, Rick Strobel, Max Volume	231-233
So Inclined	Polly Melia, John Melia, Phil Morales, Loren Higgins, Kenny Stahl	263
Solid Ground	Rene Best, Kirk Wood, Chris Schauer, Deb-bie McIntyre	
Somebody's Kids	Doug Fitz, Dave Wicks, Kurtis Mitchell, Jeff Lehmann, Ted Nelson	45-48
Something Nasty	Lou Werlinger, Mike Furlong, Ray Rodarte, Laura Edison, Claudia Edison	118, 178
Sound Factor	Tommy McDowell, Dennis Tatu, Phil Rivera	185
Southern Thunder	Lou Werlinger, Will Banks	178
Stage Door Johnny	Mike Mantor, Steve Hobson, David Clark, Danny Quintana, John Cleek, Glen Anthony, Fred Myer, Scott Myer, Terry Petersen, Richard Washburn, Jerry Weems, and bunch of others!	18-26, 84, 143, 221
Starr Donaldson with...	Jo Jo Gunne, Joe Richards Group, Opera	292

Band	Members	Pages
Steel Breeze	Spike Orberg, Paul Ojeda, Rob Bickford, Bob Thompson, Rod Toner, Tommy McLean, Tami McLean	77, 78, 120
Still Cruizin'		179
Sutro Band, The	Fred Myer, Scott Myer, Danny Hull, Jerry Weems, Rich Lewis, Jackie Larr	103
Sutro Sympathy/ Symphony Orchestra	Scott Myer, Fred Myer, Chip Condon, Rob Greer, Michael Clark, Darius Javaher, Lonesome Wayne, Lynn Hughes	234, 240
Svelts, The	Kathie Terry, June Millington, Jean Millington, Cathy Carter	142
Swiveltones #3	Tommy Rivers, B.B. Morse, Harold Aceves, Johnny Fingers, Bob McNamara	193
Sybil	Ben Dixon, Quinton Maddox, Bill White	
Taxi	Gilbert Trujillo, Bob McNamara, Bobby Crews, Danny George, Michael Manning	51, 52, 301
T-Bone Stone & The Night-Crawlers	Troy "T-Bone" Stone, Bun E. Carlos	284
Teaser	Dave Clark	84
Terraplane	Jonnie G., Travis Adlington, Robert Woodington, Chad McCall, Bart Libby, Louie Palmeri	208, 220
Terry & The T-Birds	Terry Gerard, Gary Douglas, Kevin Tokarz, Roger Hoinacki, Jerry Weems, Remmel Wilson, Ed Easton	286
Tight Quarters	Spike Orberg, Paul Taylor, David Harvey, Robbie Bickford, Chris Stevens	
Tommy Bell	Tommy Bell, Billy "Stinky" Moran, Larry Bell, Mark Speights, Mick Valentino	54
Tomorrow's Eyes	Dana Andrews, Terry Engle, Cuba "Andy" Suttles, Jimmy Schoen	131
Tribal Band of Moons	Clay Wilson, Bart Lee, John Lundemo	
Tony Savage	Tony Savage	289-290
Touch, The (aka EuroTouch)	Gilbert Trujillo, Bobby Crews, Danny George, Michael Manning, Steve Hatley	50, 52, 53
Tread	Dave Staley, Bill White, Aaron Archer, Quinton Maddox, Eric Olivas	88
Tuna Boats, The	Kathy McCovey, Tami Oxford	218
Ultimates, The	Gary Nyland, Gary Sullivan, Leon Sanders, Allen Crawford	287
Undecided, The	Ralph Henson, Bob Place, Ron Franklin, Richard Henderson, Bob Daly	59
V & T Express	Lee Miles, Mike Biselli, Jim Buehler, Dave Melroy, Nigel Giddings, Rick Levy	138
Velvet Crush	Wally Walden, Darrel Lee, Greg Sample, Steve Pot	300

Contributors

This book would not have been possible if not for the generous contributions of the following friends. Thank you all for going through old scrapbooks, drawers, boxes, suitcases, computer files, etc., and also for sending emails and texts. We greatly appreciate your efforts. We should also acknowledge that we were able to access newspaper archives that helped us to fill in the gaps.

Davo Abel

Lou Allard

Ron Barron

Louie Basso

John W. Bates

Cindy Bell

Michael Biselli

Bill Blackley

Hal Buckingham

Jim Buehler

Dave Campanaro

Vince Casey

Bill Church

Dave and Christine Clark

Jerry Coleman

Daniel Cook

Cheryl Cotton

Dana Cowen

Starr Donaldson

Tom Donnelly

Wes Elliott

Hondo John Espil

Paul Filer

Randy Fisher

Michael Furlong

Tom Gardner

Terry Gerard

Skip Gillette

Greg and Shanda Golden

Mike Grover

Johnny Hammons

Rob Hanna

Steve Hatley

Michelle Herrera

Glenn Hicks

Mike Irwin

Bill Kelly

Catherine Kirk

John Kirk

Jerry Kratzmeyer

Jim and Pete L 'Angelle

Kenny and Teri Laursen

Jeff Lehmann

Michele Lundeen

John Lundemo

Eric Maginnis

Paul Manktelow

Kathy McCovey

Bob McNamara

Julie Miller

Fred Myer

Kandas Myer

Scott Myer

William B.B. Morse

Ted Nelson

Spike Orberg

Jim Olsen

Bob Place

Kirk Poole

Danny Quintana

Gary Raffanelli

Scotty Roller

Greg Rose

Ricky and Cheryl Ruiz

Greg Sample

John Sanchez

Hagen Sandoval

April Soltis

David Strelz

Rae Ann Sullivan

John Von Nolde

Christine Wacker

Gary Joe Wade

Gaynel Wadsworth

Richard Washburn

Lou and Elaine Werlinger

Al Wilkins

Glenn Williams

Debee Van Wagner

Max Volume

Scott Wroblewski

Dedicated to all of us who've been there...

"It's quarter to three
There's no one in the place except you and me..."

Made in the USA
Monee, IL
14 June 2023